W9-CLI-790

Readings in Literary Criticism 5
CRITICS ON JANE AUSTEN

Readings in Literary Criticism

CRITICS ON JANE AUSTEN

Readings in Literary Criticism

Edited by Judith O'Neill

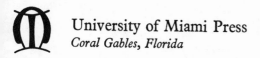

University of Miami Press
Coral Gables, Florida

CONTENTS

INTRODUCTION

Jane Austen has suffered more from her friends than her enemies. Henry James, who regarded her novels as quite rightly 'shelved and safe for all time', was disturbed by the 'beguiled infatuation' of some of her admirers whose sentimentality and undiscriminating enthusiasm were making her popular for the wrong reasons. Kipling wrote a curious story, 'The Janeites' (1926), about a little group of soldiers who suffered from this 'beguiled infatuation' and for whom the cool, ordered society and sharply defined characters had, understandably, become more real than the chaos and uncertainty of war. The student of Jane Austen certainly needs to be somewhat wary of 'Janeites' of various kinds, who gush vaguely over her person and her novels or who use her stories and characters as a convenient escape from reality, quite unaware of her own biting and satirical realism. But equally, he needs to be cautious about rushing to the other more sophisticated and fashionable extreme in Austen criticism, of reading *too* much between her lines. The valuable insights of D. W. Harding's 'Regulated Hatred' (1940), Marvin Mudrick's *Jane Austen: Irony as Defense and Discovery* (1952), Lionel Trilling's three interesting essays (1953, 1954, 1957) and Joseph M. Duffy's Freudian interpretation of *Emma* are sometimes blurred by too great an ingenuity in argument and too perverse an exegesis of her ironic intent. It is a good idea to read as widely as one can among the modern critics and not to be entirely persuaded by the first interpretation one happens to discover. Then one can gradually come to a balanced personal judgment of one's own. Whatever critical position one finally adopts, there is no doubt that Jane Austen's novels stand up to re-reading better than most. In fact, the more familiar one is with 'what happens next' and 'who marries whom', the greater the pleasure in uncovering, at each new reading, layers of hidden irony and humour that one had never seen before.

Looking back to the earlier critics of Jane Austen, there are three whose essays stand out from all others in the nineteenth century for their perceptive assessment of her work and their early opening up of crucial critical issues. They are G. H. Lewes, writing in 1859 (to whom George Eliot read all Jane Austen's novels aloud at least four times!), Julia Kavanagh in 1862, and Richard Simpson in 1870. In twentieth-century criticism, probably the three most striking landmarks have been Reginald Farrer's classic and seminal article of 1917, Mary Lascelles's detailed study *Jane Austen and Her Art* of 1939, and Marvin Mudrick's controversial but important book of 1952. The student will find any one of these three a helpful starting point for his own thinking, and he can then move on to other critics that interest him. Those who would prefer to begin by reading several critics on one novel will find *Mansfield Park* the centre of an interesting controversy. Some critics claim it to be a remarkably subtle and successful book, with touches of passion and a sensitive response to nature that set it apart from the other novels, while others see it as an interesting failure, with characters (like Mary Crawford) who quite escape from their author's intentions for them, and a pathetic heroine who suffers from too much of her author's approval. Thomas R. Edwards's article is a good introduction to all this *Mansfield Park* criticism.

Not all Jane Austen's critics have approved of her. Since Charlotte Brontë's complaint in 1848 that the novels have 'no open country, no fresh air, no blue hill, no bonny beck' to Andor Gomme's 'On not being Persuaded' in 1966, there have been a series of doubters and questioners (Garrod, Lawrence, Forster, Auden and Trilling, among others). Their criticisms of the novelist's art or of her moral values are worth taking seriously and testing by a fresh reading of the novels in their light. Any of their essays would make a good basis for group discussion.

Behind critics of all kinds stand the scholars, such as R. W. Chapman and B. C. Southam, whose patient work over many years has established the accurate and reliable texts on which all criticism must depend. In a related field of scholarship are Q. D. Leavis's important articles published in *Scrutiny* from 1941-44, which explore in detail the way Jane Austen worked and show how the finished novels emerged only gradually from early drafts and several re-writings. Mrs Leavis's 'Critical Theory' has been particularly influential over the past twenty-five years but it needs to be read today in conjunction with B. C. Southam's recent doubts about its validity. Although we have not had the space to include these discussions of textual problems or of Jane Austen's working methods or of the books and incidents that influenced her writing, students who would like to follow up these questions will find full details for further reading in the Select Bibliography at the end of this book.

Cambridge, 1970   *Judith O'Neill*

ACKNOWLEDGEMENTS

We are grateful to the following for permission to use copyright material from the works whose titles follow in brackets:

F. W. Bateson and Basil Blackwell and Mott Ltd. (C. S. Lewis's *A Note on Jane Austen*); Malcolm Bradbury (*Jane Austen's 'Emma'*); Cambridge University Press (R. A. Brower's *The Controlling Hand*; Lord David Cecil's *Jane Austen: The Leslie Stephen Lecture*; and D. W. Harding's *Regulated Hatred*); Clarendon Press, Oxford (G. K. Chesterton's *The Victorian Age in Literature* and Mary Lascelles's *Jane Austen and Her Art*); Curtis Brown Ltd. and Random House, Inc. (W. H. Auden's *Letters from Iceland*); E. M. Forster and Edward Arnold (Publishers) Ltd. (*Abinger Harvest*); Lawrence Lerner, Chatto and Windus Ltd. and Schocken Books (*The Truthtellers*); Horace Marshall and Son Ltd. (Clara Linklater Thompson's *Jane Austen: A Survey*); Marvin Mudrick (*Jane Austen: Irony as Defense and Discovery*); Mrs Willa Muir and the Hogarth Press Ltd. (Edwin Muir's *The Structure of the Novel*); John Murray (Publishers) Ltd. (Reginald Farrer's *Jane Austen, ob. July 18, 1817*); Laurence Pollinger Ltd., the Estate of the late Mrs Frieda Lawrence, Penguin Books Ltd. and the Viking Press (D. H. Lawrence's *A propos of Lady Chatterley's Lover*); The Times Publishing Co. (R. W. Chapman's *Jane Austen's Methods*); University of California Press (Thomas R. Edwards's *The Difficult Beauty of 'Mansfield Park'*); the late Leonard Woolf, the Hogarth Press and the New Statesman and Nation Publishing Co. (Leonard Woolf's *The Economic Determination of Jane Austen* and Virginia Woolf's review of Jane Austen's *Works*).

We regret we have been unable to trace the copyright holder of H. W. Garrod's *Jane Austen: A Depreciation* and would welcome any information which would enable us to do so.

Critics on Jane Austen: 1813-1939

JANE AUSTEN: 1813; 1815; 1816

Some Comments from Her Letters

... I must confess that I think [Elizabeth] as delightful a creature as ever appeared in print, and how I shall be able to tolerate those who do not like *her* at least I do not know....

> Letter to her sister Cassandra, January 29, 1813; *Jane Austen: Letters to Her Sister Cassandra and Others,* Collected and Edited by R. W. Chapman, London, 1932; 2nd ed. 1952, Letter 76, p. 297.

... [*Pride and Prejudice*] is rather too light, and bright, and sparkling; it wants shade; it wants to be stretched out here and there with a long chapter of sense, if it could be had; if not, of solemn specious nonsense, about something unconnected with the story; an essay on writing, a critique of Sir Walter Scott, or the history of Buonaparte, or anything that would form a contrast, and bring the reader with increased delight to the playfulness and epigrammatism of the general style. I doubt your quite agreeing with me here. I know your starched notions....

> Letter to her sister Cassandra, February 4, 1813; *Ibid.* Letter 77, pp. 299–300.

... My greatest anxiety at present is that this fourth work [*Emma*] should not disgrace what was good in the others. But on this point I will do myself the justice to declare that, whatever may be my wishes for its success, I am very strongly haunted with the idea that to those readers who have preferred *Pride and Prejudice* it will appear inferior in wit, and to those who have preferred *Mansfield Park* very inferior in good sense. Such as it is, however, I hope you will do me the favour of accepting a copy. Mr Murray will have directions for sending one. I am quite honoured by your thinking me capable of drawing such a clergyman as you gave the sketch of in your note of November 16th. But I assure you I am *not*. The comic part of the character I might be equal to, but not the good, the enthusiastic, the literary. Such a man's conversation must at times be on subjects of science and philosophy, of which I know nothing; or at least be occasionally abundant in quotations and allusions which a woman who, like me, knows only her own mother tongue, and has read very little in that, would be totally without the power of giving. A classical education, or at any rate a very extensive acquaintance with English literature, ancient and modern, appears to me quite indispensable for the person who would do any justice to your clergyman; and I think I may boast myself to be, with all possible vanity, the most unlearned and uninformed female who ever dared to be an authoress....

Letter to Mr James Stanier Clarke, domestic chaplain to the Prince of Wales, December 11, 1815; *Ibid.* Letter 120, p. 443.

...By the bye, my dear Edward, I am quite concerned for the loss your Mother mentions in her Letter; two Chapters and a half to be missing is monstrous! It is well that *I* have not been at Steventon lately, and therefore cannot be suspected of purloining them;—two strange twigs and a half towards a Nest of my own, would have been something.—I do not think however that any theft of that sort would be really very useful to me. What should I do with your strong, manly, spirited Sketches, full of Variety and Glow?— How could I possibly join them on to the little bit (two inches wide) of Ivory on which I work with so fine a Brush, as produces little effect after much labour?...

Letter to her nephew, J. Edward Austen, then aged 18, December 16, 1816; *Ibid.* Letter 134, pp. 468-9.

WALTER SCOTT: 1816; 1826

The First Assessment

...We...bestow no mean compliment upon the author of *Emma*, when we say that, keeping close to common incidents, and to such characters as occupy the ordinary walks of life, she has produced sketches of such spirit and originality, that we never miss the excitation which depends upon a narrative of uncommon events, arising from the consideration of minds, manners, and sentiments, greatly above our own. In this class she stands almost alone; for the scenes of Miss Edgeworth are laid in higher life, varied by more romantic incident, and by her remarkable power of embodying and illustrating national character. But the author of *Emma* confines herself chiefly to the middling classes of society; her most distinguished characters do not rise greatly above well-bred country gentlemen and ladies; and those which are sketched with most originality and precision, belong to a class rather below that standard. The narrative of all her novels is composed of such common occurrences as may have fallen under the observation of most folks; and her *dramatis personae* conduct themselves upon the motives and principles which the readers may recognize as ruling their own and that of most of their acquaintances. The kind of moral, also, which these novels inculcate, applies equally to the paths of common life....

The author's knowledge of the world, and the peculiar tact with which she presents characters that the reader cannot fail to recognize, reminds us something of the merits of the Flemish school of painting. The subjects are not often elegant, and certainly never grand; but they are finished up to nature, and with a precision which delights the reader....

[The author's merits] consist much in the force of a narrative conducted with much neatness and point, and a quiet yet comic dialogue, in which the characters of the speakers evolve themselves with dramatic effect. The faults, on the contrary, arise from the minute detail which the author's plan comprehends. Characters of folly or simplicity, such as those of old Woodhouse and Miss Bates, are ridiculous when first presented, but if too often brought forward or too long dwelt upon, their prosing is apt to become as tiresome in fiction as in real society....

An unsigned review of *Emma* in *Quarterly Review*, dated October 1815 but issued March 1816, Vol. XIV, pp. 193, 197, 199–200 (188–201). The page numbers before the brackets are those of the extracts themselves; those within the brackets indicate the beginning and end of the whole article, essay or chapter from which the extracts are taken.

...Also read again and for the third time at least Miss Austen's very finely written novel of *Pride and Prejudice*. That young lady had a talent for describing the involvement and feelings and characters of ordinary life which is to me the most wonderful I ever met with. The Big Bow-wow strain I can do myself like any now going, but the exquisite touch which renders ordinary commonplace things and characters interesting from the truth of the description and the sentiment is denied to me. What a pity such a gifted creature died so early!

Journal entry, March 14, 1826; *Journal of Walter Scott 1825-6*, ed. J. G. Tait, Edinburgh, 1939, p. 135.

HENRY AUSTEN: 1817
A Brother's Personal Comment

...Of personal attractions she possessed a considerable share. Her stature was that of true elegance. It could not have been increased without exceeding the middle height. Her carriage and deportment were quiet, yet graceful. Her features were separately good. Their assemblage produced an unrivalled expression of that cheerfulness, sensibility, and benevolence, which were her real characteristics.

Her complexion was of the finest texture. It might with truth be said, that her eloquent blood spoke through her modest cheek. Her voice was extremely sweet. She delivered herself with fluency and precision. Indeed she was formed for elegant and rational society, excelling in conversation as much as in composition.... She was fond of dancing, and excelled in it....

Though the frailties, foibles, and follies of others could not escape her immediate detection, yet even on their vices did she never trust herself to comment with unkindness. The affectation of candour is not uncommon; but she had no affectation. Faultless herself, as nearly as human nature can be, she always sought, in the faults of others, something to excuse, to forgive or forget. Where extenuation was impossible, she had a sure refuge in silence. She never uttered either a hasty, a silly, or a severe expression. In short, her temper was as polished as her wit.... She was tranquil without reserve or stiffness; and communicative without intrusion or self-sufficiency....

Her reading was very extensive in history and *belles lettres*; and her memory extremely tenacious. Her favourite moral writers were Johnson in prose, and Cowper in verse. It is difficult to say at what age she was not intimately acquainted with the merits and defects of the best essays and novels in the English language. Richardson's power of creating, and preserving the consistency of his characters, as particularly exemplified in *Sir Charles Grandison*, gratified the natural discrimination of her mind, whilst her taste secured her from the errors of his prolix style and tedious narrative. She did not rank any work of Fielding quite so high. Without the slightest affectation she recoiled from everything gross. Neither nature, wit, nor humour, could make her amends for so very low a scale of morals.

Her power of inventing characters seems to have been intuitive, and almost unlimited. She drew from nature; but, whatever may have been surmised to the contrary, never from individuals.

The style of her familiar correspondence was in all respects the same as that of her novels. Everything came finished from her pen; for on all subjects she had ideas as clear as the expressions were well chosen. It is not hazarding too much to say that she never dispatched a note or letter unworthy of publication.

One trait only remains to be touched on. It makes all others unimportant. She was thoroughly religious and devout; fearful of giving offence to God, and incapable of feeling it towards any fellow creature. On serious subjects she was well-instructed, both by reading and meditation, and her opinions accorded strictly with those of our Established Church.

London, December 13, 1817.

'Biographical Notice of the Author', preface to *Northanger Abbey and Persuasion*, London, 1818, pp. ix–xii, xv–xvi.

RICHARD WHATELY: 1821

'Instruction with Amusement'

... The moral lessons ... of this lady's novels, though clearly and impressively conveyed, are not offensively put forward, but spring incidentally from the circumstances of the story; they are not forced upon the reader, but he is left to collect them (though without any difficulty) for himself: hers is that unpretending kind of instruction which is furnished by real life; and certainly no author has ever conformed more closely to real life, as well in the incidents, as in the characters and descriptions. Her fables appear to us to be, in their own way, nearly faultless; they do not consist (like those of some of the writers who have attempted this kind of common-life novel writing) of a string of unconnected events which have little or no bearing on one main plot, and are introduced evidently for the sole purpose of bringing in characters and conversations; but have all that compactness of plan and unity of action which is generally produced by a sacrifice of probability: yet they have little or nothing that is not probable; the story proceeds without the aid of extraordinary accidents; the events which take place are the necessary or natural consequences of what has preceded; and yet (which is a very rare merit indeed) the final catastrophe is scarcely ever clearly foreseen from the beginning, and very often comes, upon the generality of readers at least, quite unexpected. We know not whether Miss Austin (*sic*) ever had access to the precepts of Aristotle; but there are few, if any, writers of fiction who have illustrated them more successfully. . . .

Like [Shakespeare], she shows as admirable a discrimination in the characters of fools as of people of sense; a merit which is far from common. To invent, indeed, a conversation full of wisdom or of wit, requires that the writer should himself possess ability; but the converse does not hold good: it is no fool that can describe fools well; and many who have succeeded pretty well in painting superior characters, have failed in giving individuality to those weaker ones, which it is necessary to introduce in order to give a faithful representation of real life: they exhibit to us mere folly in the abstract, forgetting that to the eye of a skilful naturalist the insects on a leaf present as wide differences as exist between the elephant and the lion. Slender and Shallow, and Aguecheek, as Shakespeare has painted them, though equally fools, resemble one another no more than Richard, and Macbeth, and Julius Caesar; and Miss Austin's Mrs Bennet, Mr Rushworth, and Miss Bates, are no more alike than her Darcy, Knightley, and Edmund Bertram. . . .

On the whole, Miss Austin's works may safely be recommended, not only as among the most unexceptionable of their class, but as combining, in an eminent degree, instruction with amusement,

though without the direct effort at the former, of which we have complained, as sometimes defeating its object. For those who cannot, or
will not, *learn* any thing from productions of this kind, she has
provided entertainment which entitles her to thanks.... Those,
again, who delight in the study of human nature, may improve in
the knowledge of it, and in the profitable application of that knowledge, by the perusal of such fictions as those before us.

Unsigned review of *Northanger Abbey and Persuasion*, in Quarterly
Review, Vol. XXIV, 1821, pp. 360, 362, 375–6 (352–76).

THOMAS BABINGTON MACAULAY: 1843

'Nearest to Shakespeare'

... Shakespeare had had neither equal nor second. But among
the writers who, in the point which we have noticed, have approached
nearest to the manner of the great master, we have no hesitation in
placing Jane Austen, a woman of whom England is justly proud. She
has given us a multitude of characters, all, in a certain sense,
common-place, all such as we meet every day. Yet they are all as
perfectly discriminated from each other as if they were the most
eccentric of human beings. There are, for example, four clergymen,
none of whom we should be surprised to find in any parsonage in the
kingdom, Mr Edward Ferrars, Mr Henry Tilney, Mr Edmund
Bertram, and Mr Elton. They are all specimens of the upper part
of the middle class. They have all been liberally educated. They all
lie under the restraints of the same sacred profession. They are all
young. They are all in love. Not one of them has any hobbyhorse,
to use the phrase of Sterne. Not one has a ruling passion, such as we
read of in Pope. Who would not have expected them to be insipid
likenesses of each other? No such thing. Harpagon is not more unlike
to Jourdain, Joseph Surface is not more unlike to Sir Lucius O'Trigger,
than every one of Miss Austen's young divines to all his reverend
brethren. And almost all this is done by touches so delicate, that
they elude analysis, that they defy the powers of description, and
that we know them to exist only by the general effect to which they
have contributed....

'Diary and Letters of Madame D'Arblay', an unsigned article in
Edinburgh Review, Vol. LXXVI, January 1843, pp. 561–2 (530–70).

CHARLOTTE BRONTË: 1848; 1850

'A Most Sensible Lady'

... Why do you like Miss Austen so very much? I am puzzled on
that point. What induced you to say that you would have rather

written *Pride and Prejudice* or *Tom Jones*, than any of the Waverley Novels?

I had not seen *Pride and Prejudice* till I read that sentence of yours, and then I got the book. And what did I find? An accurate daguerreotyped portrait of a commonplace face; a carefully fenced, highly cultivated garden, with neat borders and delicate flowers; but no glance of a bright, vivid physiognomy, no open country, no fresh air, no blue hill, no bonny beck. I should hardly like to live with her ladies and gentlemen, in their elegant but confined houses. These observations will probably irritate you, but I shall run the risk. . . .

Letter to G. H. Lewes, January 12, 1848; *The Brontës: Their Friendships, Lives, and Correspondence*, eds. T. J. Wise and J. A. Symington, Oxford, 1932, Vol. II, pp. 179-80.

. . . She does her business of delineating the surface of the lives of genteel English people curiously well; there is a Chinese fidelity, a miniature delicacy in the painting: she ruffles her reader by nothing vehement, disturbs him by nothing profound: the Passions are perfectly unknown to her; she rejects even a speaking acquaintance with that stormy Sisterhood; even to the Feelings she vouchsafes no more than an occasional graceful but distant recognition; too frequent converse with them would ruffle the smooth elegance of her progress. Her business is not half so much with the human heart as with the human eyes, mouth, hands and feet; what sees keenly, speaks aptly, moves flexibly, it suits her to study, but what throbs fast and full, though hidden, what the blood rushes through, what is the unseen seat of Life and the sentient target of death—this Miss Austen ignores; she no more, with her mind's eye, beholds the heart of her race than each man, with bodily vision sees the heart in his heaving breast. Jane Austen was a complete and most sensible lady, but a very incomplete, and rather insensible (*not senseless*) woman, if this is heresy—I cannot help it. . . .

Letter to W. S. Williams, April 12, 1850; *Ibid.* Vol. III, p. 99.

GEORGE HENRY LEWES: 1859

A Great Victorian Assessment of Jane Austen

. . . We have re-read [Jane Austen's novels] all four times; or rather, to speak more accurately, they have been read aloud to us, one after the other; and when it is considered what a severe test that is, how the reading aloud permits no skipping, no evasion of weariness, but brings both merits and defects into stronger relief by forcing the mind to dwell on them, there is surely something significant of genuine excellence when both reader and listener finish their fourth reading with increase of admiration. The test of reading aloud applied to *Jane Eyre*, which had only been read once before, very considerably modified our opinion of that remarkable work; and, to confess the truth, modified it so far that we feel as if we should never open the book again. . . .

While other writers have had more power over the emotions, more vivid imaginations, deeper sensibilities, deeper insight, and more of what is properly called invention, no novelist has approached her in what we may style the 'economy of art', by which is meant the easy adaptation of means to ends, with no aid from extraneous or superfluous elements. . . . It is easy for the artist to choose a subject from every-day life, but it is *not* easy for him so to represent the characters and their actions that they shall be at once lifelike and interesting; accordingly, whenever ordinary people are introduced, they are either made to speak a language never spoken out of books, and to pursue conduct never observed in life; or else they are intolerably wearisome. But Miss Austen is like Shakespeare: she makes her very noodles inexhaustibly amusing, yet accurately real. We never tire of her characters. They become equal to actual experiences. They live with us, and form perpetual topics of comment. We have so personal a dislike to Mrs Elton and Mrs Norris, that it would gratify our savage feeling to hear of some calamity befalling them. We think of Mr Collins and John Thorpe with such a mixture of ludicrous enjoyment and angry contempt, that we alternately long and dread to make their personal acquaintance. The heroines—at least Elizabeth, Emma, and Catherine Morland—are truly *lovable,* flesh-and-blood young women; and the good people are all really good, without being goody. . . . She seldom describes anything, and is not felicitous when she attempts it. But instead of *description,* the common and easy resource of novelists, she has the rare and difficult art of *dramatic presentation*: instead of telling us what her characters are, and what they feel, she presents the people, and they reveal themselves. In this she has never perhaps been surpassed, not even by Shakespeare himself. If ever living beings can be said to have moved across the page of fiction, as they lived, speaking as they spoke, and feeling as they felt, they do so in *Pride and Prejudice, Emma,* and *Mansfield Park.* What incomparable noodles she exhibits for our astonishment and laughter! What silly, good-natured women! What softly-selfish men! What lively, amiable, honest men and women, whom one would rejoice to have known!

But all her power is dramatic power; she loses her hold on us directly she ceases to speak through the *personae;* she is then like a great actor *off* the stage. When she is making men and women her mouth-pieces, she is exquisitely and inexhaustibly humorous; but when she speaks in her own person, she is apt to be commonplace, and even prosing. Her dramatic ventriloquism is such that, amid our tears of laughter and sympathetic exasperation at folly, we feel it almost impossible that she did not hear those very people utter those very words. In many cases this was doubtless the fact. The best invention does not consist in finding *new* language for characters, but in finding the *true* language for them. It is easy to invent a language never spoken by any one out of books; but it is so far from easy to invent—that is, to find out—the language which certain characters would speak and did speak. . . .

It is probably this same dramatic instinct which makes the construction of her stories so admirable. And by construction, we mean the art which, selecting what is useful and rejecting what is superfluous, renders our interest unflagging, because one chapter evolves the next, one character is necessary to the elucidation of another. In what is commonly called 'plot' she does not excel. Her invention is wholly in character and motive, not in situation. Her materials are of the commonest every-day occurrence. Neither the emotions of tragedy, nor the exaggerations of farce, seem to have the slightest attraction for her. The reader's pulse never throbs, his curiosity is never intense; but his interest never wanes for a moment. The action begins; the people speak, feel, and act; everything that is said, felt, or done tends towards the entanglement or disentanglement of the plot; and we are almost made actors as well as spectators of the little drama. . . .

So entirely dramatic, and so little descriptive, is the genius of Miss Austen, that she seems to rely upon what her people say and do for the whole effect they are to produce on our imaginations. She no more thinks of describing the physical appearance of her people than the dramatist does who knows that his persons are to be represented by living actors. This is a defect and a mistake in art: a defect, because, although every reader must necessarily conjure up to himself a vivid image of people whose characters are so vividly presented; yet each reader has to do this for himself without aid from the author, thereby missing many of the subtle connections between physical and mental organization. It is not enough to be told that a young gentleman had a fine countenance and an air of fashion; or that a young gentlewoman was handsome and elegant. As far as any direct information can be derived from the authoress, we might imagine that this was a purblind world, wherein nobody ever saw anybody, except in a dim vagueness which obscured all peculiarities. It is impossible that Mr Collins should not have been endowed by nature with an appearance in some way heralding the delicious folly of the inward man. Yet *all* we hear of this fatuous curate is, that 'he was a tall heavy-looking young man of five-and-twenty. His air was grave and stately, and his manners were very formal.' Balzac or Dickens would not have been content without making the reader *see* this Mr Collins. Miss Austen is content to make us *know* him, even to the very intricacies of his inward man. It is not stated whether she was shortsighted, but the absence of all sense of the outward world—either scenery or personal appearance —is more remarkable in her than in any writer we remember.

We are touching here on one of her defects which help to an explanation of her limited popularity, especially when coupled with her deficiences in poetry and passion. She has little or no sympathy with what is picturesque and passionate. This prevents her from painting what the popular eye can see, and the popular heart can feel. . . .

We have endeavoured to express the delight which Miss Austen's works have always given us, and to explain the sources of her success by indicating the qualities which make her a model worthy of the study of all who desire to understand the art of the novelist. But we have also indicated what seem to be the limitations of her genius, and to explain why it is that this genius, moving only amid the quiet scenes of every-day life, with no power over the more stormy and energetic activities which find vent even in every-day life, can never give her a high rank among great artists. Her place is among great artists, but it is not high among them. She sits in the House of Peers, but it is as a simple Baron. The delight derived from her pictures arises from our sympathy with ordinary characters, our relish of humour, and our intellectual pleasure in art for art's sake. But when it is admitted that she never stirs the deeper emotions, that she never fills the soul with a noble aspiration, or brightens it with a fine idea, but, at the utmost, only teaches us charity for the ordinary failings of ordinary people, and sympathy with their goodness, we have admitted an objection which lowers her claims to rank among the great benefactors of the race; and this sufficiently explains why, with all her excellence, her name has not become a household word. Her fame, we think, must endure. Such art as hers can never grow old, never be superseded. But, after all, miniatures are not frescoes, and her works are miniatures. Her place is among the Immortals; but the pedestal is erected in a quiet niche of the great temple.

'The Novels of Jane Austen', an unsigned article in *Blackwood's Edinburgh Magazine*, Vol. LXXXVI, July 1859, pp. 100, 102, 104–6, 112–13 (99–113).

JULIA KAVANAGH: 1862

Jane Austen's Strengths and Limitations

. . . Beyond any other of Miss Austen's tales, *Persuasion* shows us the phase of her literary character which she chose to keep most in the shade: the tender and the sad. In this work, as in *Sense and*

Sensibility, and in *Mansfield Park,* but with more power than in either, she showed what can be the feelings of a woman compelled to see the love she most longs for, leaving her day by day. The judicious Elinor is, indeed, conscious that she is beloved; but her lover is not free, and she long thinks him lost. Fanny is her lover's *confidante,* and must be miserable when he is blest, or happy when he is wretched. The position of Anne Elliot has something more desolate still. The opposition of her relatives, and the advice of friends, induce her to break with a young naval officer, Captain Frederick Wentworth, to whom she is engaged, and the only man whom she can love. They part, he in anger, she in sorrow; he to rise in his profession, become a rich man, and outlive his grief; she to pine at home, and lose youth and beauty in unavailing regret. Years have passed when they meet again. Captain Wentworth is still young, still handsome and agreeable. He wishes to marry, and is looking for a wife. Anne Elliot, pale, faded, and sad, knows it, and sees it—she sees the looks, the smiles of fresher and younger beauties seeking him, and apparently not seeking him in vain.

Here we see the first genuine picture of that silent torture of an unloved woman, condemned to suffer thus because she is a woman and must not speak, and which, many years later, was wakened into such passionate eloquence by the author of *Jane Eyre.* Subdued though the picture is in Miss Austen's pages, it is not the less keen, not the less painful. The tale ends happily. Captain Wentworth's coldness yields to old love, Anne's beauty returns, they are married, yet the sorrowful tone of the tale is not effaced by that happy close. The shadow of a long disappointment, of secret grief, and ill-repressed jealousy will ever hang over Anne Elliot.

This melancholy cast, the result, perhaps, of some secret personal disappointment, distinguishes *Persuasion* from Miss Austen's other tales. They were never cheerful, for even the gentlest of satire precludes cheerfulness; but this is sad.

Of the popularity of Miss Austen's six novels, of the estimation in which they are held, we need not speak. It is honourable to the public that she should be so thoroughly appreciated, not merely by men like Sir Walter Scott and Lord Macaulay, but by all who take up her books for mere amusement. Wonderful, indeed, is the power that out of materials so slender, out of characters so imperfectly marked, could fashion a story. This is her great, her prevailing merit, and yet, it cannot be denied, it is one that injures her with many readers. It seems so natural that she should have told things and painted people as they are, so natural and so easy, that we are apt to forget the performance in the sense of its reality. The literary taste of the majority is always tinged with coarseness; it loves exaggeration, and slights the modesty of truth.

Another of Miss Austen's excellencies is also a disadvantage. She does not paint or analyze her characters; they speak for themselves. Her people have never those set sayings or phrases which we may refer to the author, and of which we may think, how clever! They talk as people talk in the world, and quietly betray their inner being in their folly, falsehood, or assumption. For instance, Sir Walter Elliot is handsome; we are merely told so; but we never forget it, for he does not. He considers men born to be handsome, and, deploring the fatal effect of a seafaring life on manly beauty, he candidly regrets that 'naval gentlemen are not knocked on the head at once', so disgusted has he been with Admiral Baldwin's mahogany complexion and dilapidated appearance. And this worship of personal appearance is perfectly unaffected and sincere. Sir Walter Elliot's good looks have acted on him internally; his own daughter Anne rises in his opinion as her complexion grows clearer, and his first inquiry concerning his married daughter, Mary, is 'How is she looking?' The last time he, Sir Walter, saw her, she had a red nose, and he hopes that may not happen every day. He is assured that the red nose must have been accidental, upon which the affectionate father exclaims kindly: 'If I thought it would not tempt her to go out in sharp winds, and grow coarse, I would send her a new hat and pelisse.'

But it was natural that powers so great should fail somewhere, and there were some things which Miss Austen could not do. She could not speak the language of any strong feeling, even though that feeling were ridiculous and unjust. A rumour of Mr Darcy's marriage with Elizabeth Bennet having reached his aunt, Lady Catherine de Bourgh, she hurries down to Longbourn to tax and upbraid Miss Bennet with her audacity, and to exact from her a promise that she will not marry Mr Darcy. Elizabeth refuses, and there is a scene, but not a good one. Lady Catherine's interference is insolent and foolish, but it is the result of a strong feeling, and, to her, it is an important, a mighty matter, and this we do not feel as we read. Her assertions of her own importance, her surprise at Elizabeth's independence, are in keeping, but we want something more, and that something never appears. The delicate mind that could evolve, so shrewdly, foolishness from its deepest recesses, was powerless when strong feelings had to be summoned. They heard her, but did not obey the call.

This want of certain important faculties is the only defect, or rather causes the only defect, of Miss Austen's works: that everything is told in the same tone. An elopement, a death, seduction, are related as placidly as a dinner or ball, but with much less spirit. As she is, however, we must take her, and what her extraordinary powers wanted in extent, they made up in depth. In her own range, and admitting her cold views of life to be true, she is faultless, or almost faultless. By choosing to be all but perfect, she sometimes became monotonous, but rarely. The value of light and shade, as a means of success, she discarded. Strong contrasts, bold flights, she shunned. To be true, to show life in its everyday aspect, was her ambition. To hope to make so much out of so little showed no common confidence in her own powers, and more than common daring. Of the thousands who take up a pen to write a story meant to amuse, how many are there who can, or who dare, be true, like Jane Austen?

English Women of Letters, London, 1862; 1863 edition in 2 vols., Vol. II, Chap. VII, pp. 230-6 (218-36).

MRS (MARGARET) OLIPHANT: 1870

'The Fine Vein of Feminine Cynicism'

... Mr Austen Leigh, without meaning it, throws out of his dim little lantern a passing gleam of light upon the fine vein of feminine cynicism which pervades his aunt's mind. It is something altogether different from the rude and brutal male quality that bears the same name. It is the soft and silent disbelief of a spectator who has to look at a great many things without showing any outward discomposure, and who has learned to give up any moral classification of social sins, and to place them instead on the level of absurdities. She is not surprised or offended, much less horror-stricken or indignant, when her people show vulgar or mean traits of character, when they make it evident how selfish and self-absorbed they are, or even when they fall into those social cruelties which selfish and stupid people are so often guilty of, not without intention, but yet without the power of realizing half the pain they inflict. She stands by and looks on, and gives a soft half-smile, and tells the story with an exquisite sense of its ridiculous side, and fine stinging yet soft-voiced contempt for the actors in it. She sympathizes with the sufferers, yet she can scarcely be said to be sorry for them; giving them unconsciously a share in her own sense of the covert fun of the scene, and gentle disdain of the possibility that meanness and folly and stupidity could ever really wound any rational creature. The position of mind is essentially feminine, and one which may be readily identified in the personal knowledge of most people.... A certain soft despair of any one human creature ever doing any good to another—of any influence overcoming those habits and moods and peculiarities of mind which the observer sees to be more obstinate than life itself—a sense that nothing is to be done but to look on, to say perhaps now and then a softening word, to make the best of it practically and theoretically, to smile and hold up one's hands and wonder why human creatures should be such fools,—such are the

foundations upon which the feminine cynicism which we attribute
to Miss Austen is built. It includes a great deal that is amiable, and
is full of toleration and patience, and that habit of making allowance
for others which lies at the bottom of all human charity. But yet it
is not charity, and its toleration has none of the sweetness which
proceeds from that highest of Christian graces. It is not absolute
contempt either, but only a softened tone of general disbelief—amusement, nay enjoyment, of all those humours of humanity which are so
quaint to look at as soon as you dissociate them from any rigid standard of right or wrong. Miss Austen is not the judge of the men
and women she collects round her. She is not even their censor to
mend their manners; no power has constituted her her brother's
keeper. She has but the faculty of seeing her brother clearly all round
as if he were a statue, identifying all his absurdities, quietly jeering
at him, smiling with her eyes without committing the indecorum of
laughter. . . .

Mr Collins . . . is one of the most distinct and original portraits in
the great gallery of fiction, and we accept him gladly as a real contribution to our knowledge of humankind; not a contribution certainly
which will make us more in love with our fellow-creatures, but yet so
lifelike, so perfect and complete, touched with so fine a wit and so
keen a perception of the ridiculous, that the picture once seen
remains a permanent possession. And when we are told that the
Bennet family, with all its humours—the father who is so good and
sensible, and yet such an unmitigated bear; the mother whom he
despises and ridicules without hesitation, even to his heroine-
daughters who accept his sarcastic comments as the most natural
thing in the world; the stupid pompous Mary, the loud and noisy,
heartless and shameless Lydia—are all drawn with an equally fine
and delicate touch, we have not a word to say against it. We acknowledge its truth, and yet we rebel against this pitiless perfection of
art. It shocks us as much as it could possibly have shocked Mr
Darcy, to allow that these should be the immediate surroundings of
the young woman whom we are called upon to take to our hearts.
We blush for the daughter who blushes for her mother. We hate the
lover who points out to her, even in self-defence, the vulgarities and
follies of her family. A heroine must be superior, it is true, but not
so superior as this; and it detracts ever so much from the high
qualities of Elizabeth when we see how very ready she is to be
moved by a sense of the inferiority of her mother and sisters, how
ashamed she is of their ways, and how thankful to think that her
home will be at a distance from theirs. . . .

'Miss Austen and Miss Mitford', an unsigned review of J. E.
Austen-Leigh's *Memoir of Jane Austen, Blackwood's Edinburgh
Magazine*, Vol. CVII, March 1870, pp. 294–5, 301 (290–313).

RICHARD SIMPSON: 1870

Jane Austen's Fools

... Her biographer refers to her fools as a class of characters in delineating which she has quite caught the knack of Shakespeare. It is a natural class, better defined than most natural classes are, and less difficult to analyze. It ought therefore to serve very well to test her manner of working. In reality her fools are not more simple than her other characters. Her wisest personages have some dash of folly in them, and her least wise have something to love. And there is a collection of absurd persons in her stultifera navis, quite sufficient to make her fortune as a humourist. She seems to have considered folly to consist in two separate qualities: first, a thorough weakness either of will or intellect, an emptiness or irrelevancy of thought, such as to render it impossible to know what the person would think of any given subject, or how he would act under it; and often, secondly, in addition to this, fixed ideas on a few subjects, giving the whole tone to the person's thoughts so far as he thinks at all, and constituting the ground of the few positive judgments arrived at, even in subject-matter to which the ideas in question are scarcely related. The novels do not give a single instance of the fool simple in all the purity of its idea. Mrs Palmer, in *Sense and Sensibility*, comes the nearest to it, but in her case her thorough womanly good-nature gives a solid nucleus to a character which in order to be perfect ought to have only pepo loco cordis, a pumpkin for a heart. Intellectually however she is a nullity; and Miss Austen's method of positively representing a mere negative is ingenious and happy. It is one solution of the great problem of art, the universal form of which is, how to represent the realities of the natural scale in the imitations of the artificial scale—how to imitate the song of birds on the gamut of the pianoforte, or the coloured lights of nature with the unluminous colours of the palette. Mrs Palmer's nullity is represented first by her total want of intellectual discrimination. Her good-nature furnishes her with a perpetual smile; and any event, any word, that should cause either pain or pleasure to a person of sense, has no other effect upon her than to broaden the smile into a laugh. When she talks, her entire want of discrimination is shown in her failure to see the contradiction of contradictories. Her indignant speech about Willoughby is a typical utterance:— 'She was determined to drop his acquaintance immediately, and she was very thankful that she had never been acquainted with him at all. She wished with all her heart that Combe Magna [Willoughby's place] was not so near Cleveland [her husband's], but it did not signify, for it was a great deal too far off to visit; she hated him so much that she was resolved never to mention his name again, and she should tell everybody she saw how good-for-nothing he was.' There are foolish sayings of which a clever man might be proud; if any real Mrs Palmer could in fact string together contradictions so readily she would soon lose her character as a mere simpleton. The method does not make Mrs Palmer look so thoroughly inane as she is intended to be. . . .

In the later novel, *Emma*, where perhaps Miss Austen perfects her processes for painting humorous portraits, the negative fool is much better represented in Miss Bates. Miss Bates has enough of womanly kindness and other qualities to make her a real living person, even a good Christian woman. But intellectually she is a negative fool. She has not mind enough to fall into contradictions. There is a certain logical sequence and association between two contradictories, which it requires mind to discover: Miss Bates's fluent talk only requires memory. She cannot distinguish the relations between things. If she is standing in a particular posture when she hears a piece of news, her posture becomes at once a part of the event which it is her duty to hand down to tradition: 'Where could you possibly hear it? For it is not five minutes since I received Mrs Cole's note—no, it cannot be more than five—or at least ten—for I had got my bonnet and spencer on just ready to come out—I was only gone down to speak to Patty again about the pork—Jane was standing in the passage—were you not, Jane?—for my mother was so afraid that we had not any salting-pan large enough,' etc. etc., for it might go on for ever. Any reader can see that here is the same fortuitous concourse of details which makes up Mrs Quickly's description of Falstaff's promising her marriage—the sea-coal fire, and the green wound, and the dish of prawns—in the speech which Coleridge so justly contrasts with Hamlet's equally episodical, but always relevant, narrative of his voyage towards England.

The fool simple is soon exhausted; but when a collection of fixed ideas is grafted upon him he becomes a theme for endless variations. Mrs Bennet, in *Pride and Prejudice*, Miss Austen's earliest work, is one of this kind. She is no sooner introduced than she is defined. She is 'a woman of mean understanding, little information, and uncertain temper'. That makes up the fool negative. Her positive qualities are these: 'When she was discontented, she fancied herself nervous. The business of her life was to get her daughters married; its solace was visiting and news.' Her fixed ideas of the happiness of catching any young man for any of her daughters, of the iniquity of an entail which prevented their succeeding to her husband's estate, and of her weak nerves, make up the staple of her talk, always amusing because never to the purpose. Another fool of the same novel is Mr Collins, somewhat of a caricature, and therefore easier to analyze. He is a man of mean understanding, and a bore to boot; that is, he esteems himself worthy to be always occupying a place in the notice of those with whom he associates, and he thinks it incumbent upon him always elaborately to explain his motives, and his reasons. At the same time he has some sense of the necessity of humility, and lays claim to this virtue by always speaking of himself and his belongings as 'humble', and by the most expansive display of humility towards his patrons, and towards any one of a rank above his own. To his own personal claims he adds the official claim derived from his being a rector in the Church of England, which gives him occasion to obtrude his advice, always wrong, in the various vicissitudes of the tale. The contrast between his empty head and heart and his fixed ideas constitutes the diversion of the portrait. He is perfect when he exhorts a father to forgive his erring daughter like a Christian, and never to speak to her again.

However good these characters may be, it cannot be denied that they have in them much of the element of farce. Miss Austen in her later series of novels has given us new and improved versions of them; for example, Mr Woodhouse in *Emma*, a mere white curd of asses' milk, but still a man with humanity enough in him to be loveable in spite of, nay partly because of, his weakness and foolishness. His understanding is mean enough. His invalid's fixed ideas, which divide all that is into two kinds, wholesome and unwholesome, his notion of the superiority of his own house and family to all other houses and families, his own doctor to all other doctors, and his pork to all other pork, and his judgment of all proposals and events by their effect in bringing persons nearer to, or driving them further off from, the centre of happiness which he enjoys, show that the portrait is one of the same kind as that of Mrs Bennet, but improved by the addition of a heart. In a similar way we may compare with Mr Collins Sir Walter Elliot in *Persuasion*. He is at bottom a fool, with two fixed ideas to guide all his judgments. Vain of his own rank and good looks, these two points form his scale of comparison and rule of judgment for all men and all things: 'I have two strong grounds of objection to the navy. First, as being the means of bringing persons of obscure birth into undue distinction, and raising men to honours which their fathers and grandfathers never dreamed of; and, secondly, as it cuts up a man's youth and vigour most horribly; a sailor grows old sooner than any other man.' Sir Walter is a character constructed in the same way as Mr Collins, with simpler means and less caricature. Altogether, he is a less factitious and artificial personage than Mr Collins, who is rather built on the lines habitually adopted by Mr Dickens. Miss Austen, in her earlier fools, seems scarcely as yet to have realized the Aristotelian maxim that all things, even stones, fishes, and fools, pursue their proper end. Now, Mr Collins's fixed ideas have nothing to do with his objects in life. They govern his talk and his behaviour, but not his conduct. Sir Walter Elliot, however, is superior to Mr Collins in making his ideas his rule of life; so his portrait becomes equal in absurdity, but superior in naturalness.

There is another class of fools whom Miss Austen treats with special distinction. These people are sometimes acute enough mentally; the meanness is in their moral understanding rather than in their intellect. The conversation between John Dashwood and his wife in the opening of *Sense and Sensibility*, where she proves to him that his promises of generous conduct to his sisters, made to his dying father, do not require him to deprive himself or his children of anything that would otherwise be theirs, becomes in Miss Austen's humorous narrative a melancholy masterpiece of stupid casuistry, without conscience to build on, and of the surreptitious substitution of interest for duty. Again, Miss Thorpe the flirt, and young Thorpe the fast Oxford man, in *Northanger Abbey*, are fools rather on their moral than on their intellectual side. But in the earlier novels there is no such systematic attempt to connect wickedness with a deficiency of moral understanding as there is in the later ones. There is no endeavour to show that Wickham, the villain of *Pride and Prejudice*, or Willoughby, the villain of *Sense and Sensibility*, lacks the understanding of what virtue is. But in the much more subtle portraits of Crawford and his sister, in *Mansfield Park*, it is brought home to us throughout that their levity and want of principle is an ignorance—that, in spite of their intellectual brilliancy and good-nature, there is a want of moral understanding, analogous to the want of intelligence in the fool. So Mrs Norris, in *Mansfield Park*, a bustling, managing, sharp, and odious woman, proves to be not only wrong, but also, and in a still higher degree, foolish, by the thorough collapse of her method, and the complete failure of all her undertakings. In the earlier novels wickedness is wickedness; in the later it is ignorance also....

'Jane Austen', an unsigned review of J. E. Austen-Leigh's *Memoir of Jane Austen*, *North British Review*, Vol. LII, April 1870, pp. 145–9 (129–52).

ANDREW LANG: 1886

A Letter to Jane Austen

Ah, madam, what a relief it is to come back to your witty volumes, and forget the follies of today in those of Mr Collins and of Mrs Bennet! How fine, nay, how noble is your art in its delicate reserve, never insisting, never forcing the note, never pushing the sketch into the caricature! You worked, without thinking of it, in the spirit of Greece, on a labour happily limited, and exquisitely organized....

Letters to Dead Authors, London, 1886, p. 84 (75–85).

HENRY JAMES: 1905
'Everybody's Dear Jane'

... Let me add ... that Jane Austen, with all her light felicity, leaves us hardly more curious of her process, or of the experience in her that fed it, than the brown thrush who tells his story from the garden bough; and this, I freely confess, in spite of her being one of those of the shelved and safe, for all time, of whom I should have liked to begin by talking; one of those in whose favour discrimination has long since practically operated. She is in fact a signal instance of the way it does, with all its embarrassments, at last infallibly operate. A sharp short cut, one of the sharpest and shortest achieved, in this field, by the general judgment, came out, betimes, straight at her feet. Practically overlooked for thirty or forty years after her death, she perhaps really stands there for us as the prettiest possible example of that rectification of estimate, brought about by some slow clearance of stupidity, the half-century or so is capable of working round to. This tide has risen high on the opposite shore, the shore of appreciation—risen rather higher, I think, than the high-water mark, the highest, of her intrinsic merit and interest; though I grant indeed—as a point to be made—that we are dealing here in some degree with the tides so freely driven up, beyond their mere logical reach, by the stiff breeze of the commercial, in other words of the special bookselling spirit; an eager, active, interfering force which has a great many confusions of apparent value, a great many wild and wandering estimates, to answer for. For these distinctly mechanical and overdone reactions, of course, the critical spirit, even in its most relaxed mood, is not responsible. Responsible, rather, is the body of publishers, editors, illustrators, producers of the pleasant twaddle of magazines; who have found their 'dear', our dear, everybody's dear, Jane so infinitely to their material purpose, so amenable to pretty reproduction in every variety of what is called tasteful, and in what seemingly proves to be saleable, form.

I do not, naturally, mean that she would be saleable if we had not more or less—beginning with Macaulay, her first slightly ponderous amoroso—lost our hearts to her; but I cannot help seeing her, a good deal, as in the same lucky box as the Brontës—lucky for the ultimate guerdon; a case of popularity (that in especial of the Yorkshire sisters), a beguiled infatuation, a sentimentalized vision, determined largely by the accidents and circumstances originally surrounding the manifestation of the genius—only with the reasons for the sentiment, in this latter connection, turned the other way. The key to Jane Austen's fortune with posterity has been in part the extraordinary grace of her facility, in fact of her unconsciousness: as if, at the most, for difficulty, for embarrassment, she sometimes, over her work basket, her tapestry flowers, in the spare, cool drawing-room of other days, fell a-musing, lapsed too metaphorically, as one may say, into wool-gathering, and her dropped stitches, of these pardonable, of these precious moments, were afterwards picked up as little touches of human truth, little glimpses of steady vision, little master-strokes of imagination. . . .

'The Lesson of Balzac', 1905; *Atlantic Monthly* August 1905; reprinted in *The Question of Our Speech*, London, 1905; reprinted in *The House of Fiction*, ed. Leon Edel, London, 1957, pp. 62–3 (60–85).

G. K. CHESTERTON: 1912

'Complete Common Sense'

. . . No woman later has captured the complete common sense of Jane Austen. She could keep her head, while all the after women went about looking for their brains. She could describe a man coolly; which neither George Eliot nor Charlotte Brontë could do. She knew what she knew, like a sound dogmatist: she did not know what she did not know—like a sound agnostic. . . .

Jane Austen was born before those bonds which (we are told) protected woman from truth, were burst by the Brontës or elaborately untied by George Eliot. Yet the fact remains that Jane Austen knew much more about men than either of them. Jane Austen may have been protected from truth: but it was precious little of truth that was protected from her. When Darcy, in finally confessing his faults, says, 'I have been a selfish being all my life, in practice *though not in theory*,' he gets nearer to a complete confession of the intelligent male than ever was even hinted by the Byronic lapses of the Brontës' heroes or the elaborate exculpations of George Eliot's. Jane Austen, of course, covered an infinitely smaller field than any of her later rivals; but I have always believed in the victory of small nationalities. . . .

The Victorian Age in Literature, London, 1912; 1925 edition, pp. 105, 109.

REGINALD FARRER: 1917

An Anniversary Comment

. . . The secret of her immortality is to be found in that underlying something which is the woman herself; for, of all writers, she it is who pursues truth with most utter and undeviable devotion. The real thing is her only object always. She declines to write of scenes and circumstances that she does not know at first hand; she refuses recognition, and even condonement, to all thought or emotion that conflicts with truth, or burkes it, or fails to prove pure diamond to the solvent of her acid. She is, in fact, the most merciless, though calmest, of iconoclasts; only her calm has obscured from her critics the steely quality, the inexorable rigour of her judgment. Even Butler, her nearest descendant in this generation, never seems really to have recognized his affinity. For Jane Austen has no passion, preaches no gospel, grinds no axe; standing aloof from the world, she sees it, on the whole, as silly. She has no animosity for it; but she has no affection. She does not want to better fools, or to abuse them; she simply sets herself to glean pleasure from their folly. Nothing but the first-rate in life is good enough for her tolerance; remember Anne Elliot's definition of 'good company', and her cousin's rejoinder, 'That is not good company; that is the best.'

Everything false and feeble, in fact, withers in the demure greyness of her gaze; in 'follies and nonsense, whims and inconsistencies', she finds nothing but diversion, dispassionate but pitiless. For, while no novelist is more sympathetic to real values and sincere emotion, none also is so keen on detecting false currency, or so relentless in exposing it. At times, even, her antagonism to conventionalities and shams betrays her almost to a touch of passion. Yet, if ever she seems cruel, her anger is but just impatience against the slack thought and ready-made pretences that pass current in the world and move her always to her quiet but destructive merriment; as in the famous outburst about Miss Musgrove's 'large fat sighings over a son whom alive no one had cared for'—a *cri de cœur* for which the author for once feels immediately bound to come before the curtain, to mitigate it with a quasi-apology quite devoid of either conviction or recantation. Nor will she hear of any reserves in honesty and candour; not only the truth, but the whole truth, must be vital of any character of whom she herself is to approve. Civilized urbane discretion, and assent to social falsehoods, make strong points in Anne's private distrust of William Elliot, and in Fanny's disapproval of Henry Crawford, artfully thrown in contrast as he is against the breezy impetuous young frankness of William Price.

She is consumed with a passion for the real, as apart from the realistic; and the result is that her creations, though obviously observed, are no less obviously generalized into a new identity of their own. She acknowledges no individual portrait, such as those in which alone such essentially unimaginative writers as Charlotte Brontë can deal. And in this intense preoccupation with character, she is frankly bored with events; the accident at Lyme shows how perfunctorily she can handle a mere occurrence, being concentrated all the time on the emotions that engender it, and the emotions it engenders. Her very style is the mirror of her temperament. Naturally enough, she both writes and makes her people speak an English much more flowing and lucid than is fashionable in ordinary writers and ordinary life; but, allowing for this inevitable blemish, the note of her style is the very note of her nature, in its lovely limpidity, cool

and clear and flashing as an alpine stream, without ebulliencies or
turbidness of any kind. It is not for nothing that 'rational' is almost
her highest word of praise. Good sense, in the widest meaning of the
word, is her be-all and end-all. . . .

Now we come to the Book of Books, which is the book of Emma
Woodhouse.[1] And justly so named, with Jane Austen's undeviating
flair for the exact title. For the whole thing *is* Emma; there is only
one short scene in which Emma herself is not on the stage; and that one
scene is Knightley's conversation about her with Mrs Weston. Take
it all in all, *Emma* is the very climax of Jane Austen's work; and a real
appreciation of *Emma* is the final test of citizenship in her kingdom.
For this is not an easy book to read; it should never be the beginner's
primer, nor be published without a prefatory synopsis. Only when
the story has been thoroughly assimilated, can the infinite delights and
subtleties of its workmanship begin to be appreciated, as you realize
the manifold complexity of the book's web, and find that every sentence,
almost every epithet, has its definite reference to equally unemphasized
points before and after in the development of the plot. Thus it is
that, while twelve readings of *Pride and Prejudice* give you twelve
periods of pleasure repeated, as many readings of *Emma* give you that
pleasure, not repeated only, but squared and squared again with each
perusal, till at every fresh reading you feel anew that you never
understood anything like the widening sum of its delights. But, until
you know the story, you are apt to find its movement dense and slow
and obscure, difficult to follow, and not very obviously worth the
following.

For this is *the* novel of character, and of character alone, and of
one dominating character in particular. And many a rash reader, and
some who are not rash, have been shut out on the threshold of Emma's
Comedy by a dislike of Emma herself. Well did Jane Austen know
what she was about, when she said, 'I am going to take a heroine
whom nobody but myself will much like.' And, in so far as she fails
to make people like Emma, so far would her whole attempt have to
be judged a failure, were it not that really the failure, like the loss, is
theirs who have not taken the trouble to understand what is being
attempted. Jane Austen loved tackling problems; her hardest of all,
her most deliberate, and her most triumphantly solved, is Emma.

What is that problem? No one who carefully reads the first three
opening paragraphs of the book can entertain a doubt, or need any
prefatory synopsis; for in these the author gives us quite clear warning
of what we are to see. We are to see the gradual humiliation of self-
conceit, through a long self-wrought succession of disasters, serious in
effect, but keyed in Comedy throughout. Emma herself, in fact, *is*

---

[1] 'Heavens, let me not suppose that she dares go about Emma-Woodhouseing
me!'—*Emma*, Ch. XXXIII—a typical instance of a remark which, comic in itself,
has a second comic intention, as showing Emma's own ridiculousness.

never to be taken seriously. And it is only those who have not realized this who will be 'put off' by her absurdities, her snobberies, her misdirected mischievous ingenuities. Emma is simply a figure of fun. To conciliate affection for a character, not because of its charms, but in defiance of its defects, is the loftiest aim of the comic spirit; Shakespeare achieved it with his besotted old rogue of a Falstaff, and Molière with Célimène. It is with these, not with 'sympathetic' heroines, that Emma takes rank, as the culminating figure of English high-comedy. And to attain success in creating a being whom you both love and laugh at, the author must attempt a task of complicated difficulty. He must both run with the hare and hunt with the hounds, treat his creation at once objectively and subjectively, get inside it to inspire it with sympathy, and yet stay outside it to direct laughter on its comic aspects. And this is what Jane Austen does for Emma, with a consistent sublimity so demure that indeed a reader accustomed only to crude work might be pardoned for missing the point of her innumerable hints, and actually taking seriously, for example, the irony with which Emma's attitude about the Coles' dinner-party is treated, or the even more convulsing comedy of Emma's reflexions after it. But only Jane Austen is capable of such oblique glints of humour; and only in *Emma* does she weave them so densely into her kaleidoscope that the reader must be perpetually on his guard lest some specially delicious flash escape his notice, or some touch of dialogue be taken for the author's own intention.

Yet, as Emma really does behave extremely ill by Jane Fairfax, and even worse by Robert Martin, merely to laugh would not be enough, and every disapproval would justly be deepened to dislike. But, when we realize that each machination of Emma's, each imagined piece of penetration, is to be a thread in the snare woven unconsciously by herself for her own enmeshing in disaster, then the balance is rectified again, and disapproval can lighten to laughter once more. For this is another of Jane Austen's triumphs here—the way in which she keeps our sympathies poised about Emma. Always some charm of hers is brought out, to compensate some specially silly and ambitious naughtiness; and even these are but perfectly natural, in a strong-willed, strong-minded girl of only twenty-one, who has been for some four years unquestioned mistress of Hartfield, unquestioned Queen of Highbury. Accordingly, at every turn we are kept so dancing up and down with alternate rage and delight at Emma that finally, when we see her self-esteem hammered bit by bit into collapse, the nemesis would be too severe, were she to be left in the depths. By the merciful intention of the book, however, she is saved in the very nick of time, by what seems like a happy accident, but is really the outcome of her own unsuspected good qualities, just as much as her disasters had been the outcome of her own most cherished follies.

In fact, Emma is intrinsically honest (it is not for nothing that she is given so unique a frankness of outlook on life); and her brave recognition of her faults, when confronted with their results, conduces largely to the relief with which we hail the solution of the table, and laugh out loud over 'Such a heart, such a Harriet!' The remark is typical, both of Emma and of Emma's author. For this is the ripest and kindliest of all Jane Austen's work. Here alone she can laugh at people, and still like them; elsewhere her amusement is invariably salted with either dislike or contempt. *Emma* contains no fewer than four silly people, more or less prominent in the story; but Jane Austen touches them all with a new mansuetude, and turns them out as candidates for love as well as laughter. Nor is this all that must be said for Miss Bates and Mr Woodhouse. They are actually inspired with sympathy. Specially remarkable is the treatment of Miss Bates, whose pathos depends on her lovableness, and her lovableness on her pathos, till she comes so near our hearts that Emma's abrupt brutality to her on Box Hill comes home to us with the actuality of a violent sudden slap in our own face. But then Miss Bates, though a twaddle, is by no means a fool; in her humble, quiet, unassuming happiness, she is shown throughout as an essentially wise woman. For Jane Austen's mood is in no way softened to the second-rate and pretentious, though it is typical of *Emma* that Elton's full horror is only gradually revealed in a succession of tiny touches, many of them designed to swing back sympathy to Emma; even as Emma's own bad behaviour on Box Hill is there to give Jane Fairfax a lift in our sympathy at her critical moment, while Emma's repentance afterwards is just what is wanted to win us back to Emma's side again, in time for the coming catastrophe. And even Elton's 'broad handsome face', in which 'every feature works', pales before that of the lady who 'was, in short, so very ready to have him'. 'He called her Augusta; how delightful!'

Jane Austen herself never calls people she is fond of by these fancy names, but reserves them for such female cads or cats as Lydia Bennet, Penelope Clay, Selina Suckling, and 'the charming Augusta Hawkins'. It is characteristic, indeed, of her methods in *Emma*, that, though the Sucklings never actually appear, we come to know them (and miss them) as intimately as if they did. Jane Austen delights in imagining whole vivid sets of people, never on the stage, yet vital in the play; but in *Emma* she indulges herself, and us, unusually lavishly, with the Sucklings at Maple Grove, the Dixons in Ireland, and the Churchills at Enscombe. As for Frank, he is among her men what Mary Crawford is among her women, a being of incomparable brilliance, moving with a dash that only the complicated wonderfulness of the whole book prevents us from lingering to appreciate. In fact, he so dims his cold pale Jane by comparison that one wonders more than ever what he saw in her. The whole Frank-Jane intrigue, indeed, on which the story hinges, is by no means its most valuable or plausible part. But Jane Fairfax is drawn in dim tones by the author's deliberate purpose. She had to be dim. It was essential that nothing should bring the secondary heroine into any competition with Emma. Accordingly Jane Fairfax is held down in a rigid dullness so conscientious that it almost defeats another of her *raisons d'être* by making Frank's affection seem incredible.

But there is very much more in it than that. Emma is to behave so extremely ill in the Dixon matter that she would quite forfeit our sympathy, unless we were a little taught to share her unregenerate feelings for the 'amiable, upright, perfect Jane Fairfax'. Accordingly we are shown Jane Fairfax always from the angle of Emma; and, despite apparently artless words of eulogy, the author is steadily working all the time to give us just that picture of Jane, as a cool, reserved, rather sly creature, which is demanded by the balance of emotion and the perspective of the picture. It is curious indeed, how often Jane Austen repeats a favourite composition; two sympathetic figures, major and minor, set against an odious one. In practice, this always means that, while the odious is set boldly out in clear lines and brilliant colour, the minor sympathetic one becomes subordinate to the major, almost to the point of dullness. The respective positions of Emma, Jane, and Mrs Elton shed a flood of light back on the comparative paleness of Eleanor Tilney, standing in the same minor relation to Catherine, as against Isabella Thorpe; and the trouble about *Sense and Sensibility* is that, while Marianne and Elinor are similarly set against Lucy, Elinor, hypothetically the minor note to Marianne, is also, by the current and intention of the tale, raised to an equal if not more prominent position,[2] thus jangling the required chord, so faultlessly struck in *Northanger Abbey*, and in *Emma* only marred by the fact that Jane Fairfax's real part is larger than her actual sound-value can be permitted to be. . . .

'Jane Austen, *ob.* July 18, 1817', *The Quarterly Review*, Vol. CCXXVIII, July 1917, pp. 11–12, 23–8 (1–30).

R. W. CHAPMAN: 1922

'Exactness of Detail'

. . . The quality of her composition that most stands out, as characteristic and remarkable, is her extraordinary attention to exactness of detail. The accuracy in dates is only typical of a scrupulous realism in all similar things. She would not allow her niece to take her people from Dawlish to Bath in a day—'they are nearly 100 miles apart'. Her

---

[2] The first version of the book was called *Elinor and Marianne*; which quite clearly, coming from Jane Austen, shows that Elinor was meant to be the dominant figure.

visitors to Bath are never permitted to go to the theatre on concert nights, or to dance at the Lower Rooms on a Monday. It appears that the device of the hedgerow, used in *Persuasion*, was thought of for *Mansfield Park*—one imagines a conversation between Edmund and Mary, overheard by Fanny—but abandoned when she learned, on inquiry, that Northamptonshire was 'not a country of hedgerows'. She could not bring herself to use fictitious names for ships of war, and wrote to her brother asking leave to borrow some of his. . . . Miss Austen knows all the details, and gives us very few of them. . . . But such details as escape her are almost always right. . . .

'Jane Austen's Methods', *Times Literary Supplement*, February 9, 1922, p. 82 (81–2).

VIRGINIA WOOLF: 1923

Jane Austen at Sixty

Anybody who has had the temerity to write about Jane Austen is aware of two facts: first, that of all great writers she is the most difficult to catch in the act of greatness; second, that there are twenty-five elderly gentlemen living in the neighbourhood of London who resent any slight upon her genius as if it were an insult offered to the chastity of their Aunts. . . .

Let us take *Persuasion*, the last completed book, and look by its light at the novels that she might have written had she lived to be sixty. We do not grudge it him, but her brother the Admiral lived to be ninety-one.

There is a peculiar dullness and a peculiar beauty in *Persuasion*. The dullness is that which so often marks the transition stage between two different periods. The writer is a little bored. She has grown too familiar with the ways of her world. There is an asperity in her comedy which suggests that she has almost ceased to be amused by the vanities of a Sir Walter or the snobbery of a Miss Elliot. The satire is harsh, and the comedy crude. She is no longer so freshly aware of the amusements of daily life. Her mind is not altogether on her subject. But, while we feel that Jane Austen has done this before, and done it better, we also feel that she is trying to do something which she has never yet attempted. There is a new element in *Persuasion*, a quality, perhaps, that made Dr Whewell fire up and insist that it was 'the most beautiful of her works'. She is beginning to discover that the world is larger, more mysterious, and more romantic than she had supposed. We feel it to be true of herself when she says of Anne: 'She had been forced into prudence in her youth, she learned romance as she grew older—the natural sequel of an unnatural beginning.' She dwells frequently upon the beauty and the melancholy of nature. She talks of the 'influence so sweet and so sad of autumnal months in the country'. She marks 'the tawny leaves and withered hedges'. 'One does not love a place the less because one has suffered in it,' she observes. But it is not only in a new sensibility to nature that we detect the change. Her attitude to life itself is altered. She is seeing it, for the greater part of the book, through the eyes of a woman who, unhappy herself, has a special sympathy for the happiness and unhappiness of others, which, until the very end, she is forced to comment upon in silence. Therefore the observation is less of facts and more of feelings than is usual. There is an expressed emotion in the scene at the concert and in the famous talk about woman's constancy which proves not merely the biographical fact that Jane Austen had loved, but the aesthetic fact that she was no longer afraid to say so. Experience, when it was of a serious kind, had to sink very deep, and to be thoroughly disinfected by the passage of time, before she allowed herself to deal with it in fiction. But now, in 1817, she was ready. Outwardly, too, in her circumstances, a change was imminent. Her fame had grown very slowly. 'I doubt,' wrote Mr Austen Leigh, 'whether it would be possible to mention any other author of note whose personal obscurity was so complete.' Had she lived a few more years only, all that would have been altered. She would have stayed in London, dined out, lunched out, met famous people, made new friends, read, travelled, and carried back to the quiet country cottage a hoard of observations to feast upon at leisure.

And what effect would all this have had upon the six novels that Jane Austen did not write? She would not have written of crime, of passion, or of adventure. She would not have been rushed by the importunity of publishers or the flattery of friends into slovenliness or insincerity. But she would have known more. Her sense of security would have been shaken. Her comedy would have suffered. She would have trusted less (this is already perceptible in *Persuasion*) to dialogue and more to reflection to give us a knowledge of her characters. Those marvellous little speeches which sum up in a few minutes' chatter all that we need in order to know an Admiral Croft or a Mrs Musgrove for ever, that shorthand, hit-or-miss method which contains chapters of analysis and psychology, would have become too crude to hold all that she now perceived of the complexity of human nature. She would have devised a method, clear and composed as ever, but deeper and more suggestive, for conveying not only what people say, but what they leave unsaid; not only what they are, but (if we may be pardoned the vagueness of the expression) what life is. She would have stood further away from her characters, and seen them more as a group, less as individuals. Her satire, while it played less incessantly, would have been more stringent and severe. She would have been the forerunner of Henry James and of Proust—but enough. Vain are these speculations: she died 'just as she was beginning to feel confidence in her own success'.

A review of the 5-volume Oxford edition of Jane Austen's *Works, The Nation and The Athenaeum*, Vol. XXXIV, December 15, 1923, pp. 433–4; reprinted in an extended and slightly altered form in *The Common Reader*, Hogarth Press, London, 1925, pp. 180–3.

H. W. GARROD: 1928

A Depreciation

There is a time to be born and a time to die, and a time to be middle-aged and read Miss Austen.... Her letters may be described as a desert of trivialities punctuated by occasional oases of clever malice.... She could write at twenty as well, or better, or very nearly as well, as at forty.... It would be difficult to name a writer of similar eminence who possessed so little knowledge of literature and history, whose experience of life was so narrowly and so contentedly confined, whose interests were at once so acute and so small, whose ideals were so irredeemably humdrum....

A just irritation is constantly aroused in me by the monotonously subdued pitch of her ethical standards.... I refuse to call edifying in any intelligible sense works which accept as not only good, but natural, such worn and shabby institutions as simony, nepotism, and the marriage of convenience. The fact is that Miss Austen, beginning life with a temperament naturally cool and businesslike, took, not the world (which she never touches), but the parish, as she found it. There is a parochialism which is worse than worldliness.... Her situation, character and knowledge were in almost every direction absurdly limited. She is only detached where she is in fact uninformed, and silent where uninterested. She knew, and was interested in, not her own sex, but that rather small subdivision of it which was most like herself. From music, art, books, events, the beautiful in nature, social and religious interests, and from what is grand, as distinct from interesting, in human nature, she is complacently detached.... Her art shows no development ... her range never widens, her tone never deepens. She invents no new plots, she repeats her characters, she employs again and again the same setting....

A drab scenery the worse for use; a thin plot unfashionable cut, and by turning, re-lining and trimming made to do duty for five or six novels; a dozen or so stock characters—these are Miss Austen's materials.... It is true that she cannot tell a story, but it is equally true that she does not want to. Her interest is not in happenings, but in humours. Of these her perception is, to my mind, clear rather than quick, and her expression of them nicely calculated rather than subtle. It is consistent with this that her best characters are the minor ones. Her votaries must pardon me if I still find Emma an unconvincing person, and if, among her other heroines, I am happy with none save Elizabeth Bennet. I daresay there is a land of promise in which we may one day meet such young women as Fanny Price, Anne Elliot, Elinor Dashwood; but it will be a land flowing with milk and water. Miss Austen's heroes, and her bad young men, are not, I fancy, defended even by her eulogists. It may be doubted whether she herself felt at home among them. It has been observed that nowhere in any of her books does one man talk to another. Clearly Miss Austen did not know how young men do talk to one another; and it is an essential condition of her talent that she never strays outside the range of her knowledge and experience....

'Jane Austen: A Depreciation', *Essays by Divers Hands: Transactions of the Royal Society of Literature,* n.s. Vol. VIII, 1928, pp. 21, 25, 28–9, 30–2, 36–8 (21–40).

EDWIN MUIR: 1928

Character and Action in the Dramatic Novel

... In all its forms the dramatic novel need not be tragic, and the first novelist who practised it with consummate success in England—Jane Austen—consistently avoided and probably was quite incapable of sounding the tragic note. The instance may seem strange, but it is only so in appearance. The art of Jane Austen has a more essential resemblance to that of Hardy than to Fielding's or Thackeray's. There is in her novels, in the first place, a confinement to one circle, one complex of life, producing naturally an intensification of action; and this intensification is one of the essential attributes of the dramatic novel. In the second place, character is to her no longer a thing merely to delight in, as it was to Fielding, Smollett and Scott, and as it remained later to Dickens and Thackeray. It has consequences. It influences events; it creates difficulties and later, in different circumstances, dissolves them. When Elizabeth Bennet and Darcy meet first, the complexion of their next encounter is immediately determined. The action is set going by the changing tension between them and by a few acts of intervention on the part of the other figures; and the balance of all the forces within the novel creates and moulds the plot. There is no external framework, no merely mechanical plot; all is character, and all is at the same time action. One figure in the pure comedic sense there is in the book, Mr Collins. Mr Collins has no great effect on the action; he is an end, not a means and an end at the same time; he remains unchanged throughout the story. There are other pure comedic elements; for example, the permanent domestic tension between Mr and Mrs Bennet. But in most dramatic novels such figures and combinations are to be found....

Where [the] plot [of *Pride and Prejudice*] differs from the plot of a novel of action is in its strict interior causation. The first aversion of Elizabeth for Darcy was inevitable because of the circumstances in

which they met, because Darcy was proud of his social position and
Elizabeth encumbered by her unpresentable family, and because
they were people of such decided character that they were certain to
dislike each other at the beginning. Elizabeth is true to the candour
of her mind in believing Darcy to be cold, haughty and vindictive; she
is equally true to it later in acknowledging that she is mistaken, and in
changing her opinion. The action is created here by those characters
who remain true to themselves; it is their constancy which, like a law
of necessity, sets the events moving; and through these they gradually
manifest themselves.

The correspondence in a novel of this kind between the action and
the characters is so essential that one can hardly find terms to describe
it without appearing to exaggerate; one might say that a change in the
situation always involves a change in the characters, while every
change, dramatic or psychological, external or internal, is either caused
or given its form by something in both....

Coming back to *Pride and Prejudice* we may take up now the other
respect in which it diverges from the character novel; its confinement
to a narrow scene, and to one complex of life. We shall find this concentration of the area of action in almost all dramatic novels. We find
it in Hardy, in Emily Brontë, in *The House with the Green Shutters,*
even in *Moby Dick,* where though the stage is vast, it is in a sense
unchanged: there is no escape from it. The reason for the isolation
of the scene in the dramatic novel is obvious enough. Only in a completely shut-in arena can the conflicts which it portrays arise, develop,
and end inevitably. All the exits are closed, and as we watch the
action we know this. There is no escape into other scenes, or if there
is we know that they are false exits bringing the protagonist back to
the main stage again, where he must await his destiny. The scene here
is the framework within which the logic of the action can develop
unimpeded, and shut off from the arbitrary interference of the external
world. It gives necessity to that logic by defining the limits within
which it may work....

The Structure of the Novel, London, 1928, pp. 42–3, 45–8, 58–9
(41–61).

C. LINKLATER THOMPSON: 1929

The Unity of Time in the Novels

... One reason why Miss Austen's stories cohere so neatly is that she
seems always to have kept in mind a distinct period of time over
which she distributed her incidents. In *Sense and Sensibility* the action
extends from the autumn of one year till the summer of the next (Mrs
Jennings visited Edward and his wife in their parsonage by Michael-
mas); in *Pride and Prejudice* from one autumn to the next; in *Mans-*

field Park from the summer to the following spring; in *Emma* from September to July; in *Northanger Abbey* the events are distributed over eleven weeks in February, March and April; in *Persuasion* the action begins in the autumn and lasts till the following spring. Thus the period is never a long one, and she keeps so strictly to her appointed time-table that she is supposed to have had an actual calendar before her as she wrote. She seems to live from day to day with her characters; and that the reader may do this also, she is careful to remind him of the passage of time, sometimes by an actual date, and very often by an allusion to the state of the weather. In *Mansfield Park*, Fanny, wearying in her sordid Portsmouth home, thinks of the procession of spring flowers in her aunt's garden; and Anne in *Persuasion*, which opens in October, grieves to miss the autumnal beauty of the grounds of Kellynch Hall. Sometimes it is a less poetical allusion that reminds us of the season. When Mr Woodhouse entertains Mrs Goddard and Mrs Bates during his daughter's absence at Mr Weston's ball, he sends away the asparagus because it is insufficiently cooked, and the date of the party at Donwell is marked by the fact that the strawberries are ripe. Thus a kind of unity of time is preserved, though the unit is a year or less, rather than a day.

The advantage of thus compressing the action is obvious. If a long stretch of time were involved it would be impossible to present scenes and dialogues with the detail and delicacy that characterize Miss Austen's writing; some would have to be omitted, and others would have to be abridged, and the events of long periods must be summarized in the much less vivid form of narrative. As it is, we are in the daily company of her characters; it is Monday, and Mrs Bennet can provide no fish for her guest; Friday, Saturday, Sunday and Monday are wet, and Lydia cannot walk into Meryton. So Miss Austen enforces the impression of reality, and cheats us into the belief that we are sharing with the creatures of her imagination their experience of life....

Jane Austen: A Survey, London, 1929, pp. 242–3.

D. H. LAWRENCE: 1930

'This Old Maid'

... In the old England, the curious blood-connection held the classes together. The squires might be arrogant, violent, bullying and unjust, yet in some ways they were *at one* with the people, part of the same blood-stream. We feel it in Defoe or Fielding. And then, in the mean Jane Austen, it is gone. Already this old maid typifies 'personality' instead of character, the sharp knowing in apartness instead of knowing in togetherness, and she is, to my feeling, thoroughly unpleasant,

English in the bad, mean, snobbish sense of the word, just as Fielding is English in the good, generous sense. . . .

A Propos of Lady Chatterley's Lover, London, 1930, p. 58.

E. M. FORSTER: 1932
Jane Austen's Letters

. . . She wrote letters. . . . They do not draw distant ages together, like the letters which were written at the same time by Keats. They were temporary and local in their appeal, and their essential meaning went down with her into the grave. . . .

The novels are good—of that there is no doubt, and they are so good that everything connected with the novelist and everything she wrote ought certainly to be published and annotated. Of that, too there is no doubt, and this elaborate edition (*Jane Austen: Letters,* ed. R. W. Chapman, 2 vols., Oxford, 1932) is thoroughly justified. But—and here comes the dubious spot—are the letters themselves good? Very reluctantly, and in spite of Mr Chapman's quiet instigations to the contrary, one must answer 'No'. . . .

Are not most of these two volumes catalogues of trivialities which do not come alive? They were alive at the time, but they have not the magic that outlasts ink: they are the letters of Miss Austen, not of Jane Austen: and Miss Austen would think us silly to read them, for she knows that we have not and cannot have their key. When the breath left her body it was lost, though a ghost of it lingered for a time in the hands of those who had loved her. Cassandra understood, her niece Fanny Knight understood, the Austen Leighs and Lord Brabourne had some conception—but we students of today, unrelated to her by blood, what part have we in this family talk, and whose triviality do we expose but our own?

It would be incorrect to say that the letters do not suggest the novels. They suggest them constantly: the quiet houses, the miry lanes, the conundrums, the absence of the very rich and the very poor, the snobbery which flourishes where distinctions of income are slight —all are present and some of the characters are present in solution. But never the finer characters. These never seem to get uppermost when Miss Austen writes a letter. They belong to another part of her mind. Neither Emma Woodhouse nor Anne Elliot nor even Frank Churchill or Mary Crawford dominates her pen. The controls are rather Lydia Bennet, Mrs Jennings and Sir Thomas Bertram, a bizarre and inauspicious combine. . . .

Triviality, varied by touches of ill breeding and of sententiousness, characterizes these letters as a whole, particularly the earlier letters; and certain critics of weight, Mr Chapman among them, find the triviality delightful, and rightly point out that there is a charm in little things. Yes, when it is the charm of Cowper. But the little things must hold out their little hands to one another; and here there is a scrappiness which prevents even tartness from telling. This brings us to the heart of the matter, to Miss Austen's fundamental weakness as a letter-writer. She has not enough subject-matter on which to exercise her powers. . . . When she writes a letter she has nothing in her mind except the wish to tell her sister everything; and so she flits from the cows to the currant bushes, from the currant bushes to Mrs Hall of Sherborne, gives Mrs Hall a tap and flits back again. She suffers from a poverty of material which did no injury to the novels and indeed contributes to their triumph. Miss Bates may flit and Mrs Norris tap as much as they like, because they do so inside a frame which has been provided by a great artist, and Meryton may reproduce the atmosphere of Steventon because it imports something else—some alignment not to be found on any map. . . .

After all, whatever feeling we hold about her, we must agree that the supreme thing in life to her was the family. She knew no other allegiance; if there was an early love affair in the west of England, and if her lover died, as did her sister Cassandra's, she never clung to his memory, unless she utilizes it in *Persuasion*. Intimacy out of the unknown never overwhelmed her. No single person ever claimed her. She was part of a family, and her dearest Cassandra only the dearest in that family. The family was the unit within which her heart had liberty of choice; friends, neighbours, plays and fame were all objects to be picked up in the course of a flight outside and brought back to the nest for examination. They often laughed over the alien trophies, for they were a hard humorous family. And these letters, however we judge them on their own count, are invaluable as a document. They show, more clearly than ever, that Miss Austen was part of the Austens, the Knights, the Leighs, the Lefroys. The accidents of birth and relationship were more sacred to her than anything else in the world, and she introduces this faith as the groundwork of her six great novels.

Review in *Times Literary Supplement*, November 10, 1932, pp. 821–2. Reprinted in *Abinger Harvest*, London, 1936, pp. 153–9 (152–9).

LORD DAVID CECIL: 1935

The Moral-Realistic View of Life

. . . Like all great comedians, she satirizes in relation to a universal standard of values: her books express a general view of life. It is the view of that eighteenth-century civilization of which she was the last exquisite blossom. One might call it the moral-realistic view. Jane Austen was profoundly moral. She thought you lived only to be good, that it was the first duty of everyone to be sincere, unselfish and disinterested. But the very seriousness with which she held this conviction made her think it imperative to see life realistically. Good notions were to be acted upon; therefore you could only be sure they were good if they passed the test of commonsense and experience. She despised all ideals, however lofty, that were not practical, all emotions, however soul-stirring, if they did not in fact make for the benefit and happiness of mankind. Indeed she did not value emotions as such at all. She reserved some of her most mischievous mockery for extravagant maternal affection and sentimental rhapsodizing over nature. Love itself, though she understood its workings admirably, did not rouse her enthusiasm unless it was justified by reason, disciplined by self-control. She had little sympathy for romantic imprudence or credulous good nature; she was impatient of people with hearts of gold and heads of wood. And though she was not a slave to worldly considerations she thought it a mistake to overlook them entirely. It was wrong to marry for money, but it was silly to marry without it. Nor should one lightly break with convention. Only fools imagined they could live happily in the world without paying attention to what its inhabitants thought. . . .

Jane Austen: The Leslie Stephen Lecture, 1935, Cambridge, 1935, pp. 21–2, 32–3, 41–2.

W. H. AUDEN: 1937

'*You could not shock her more than she shocks me*'

You could not shock her more than she shocks me;
Beside her Joyce seems innocent as grass.
It makes me most uncomfortable to see
An English spinster of the middle-class
Describe the amorous effects of 'brass',
Reveal so frankly and with such sobriety
The economic basis of society.

'Letter to Lord Byron, Part I', in W. H. Auden and Louis MacNeice, *Letters from Iceland,* Faber and Faber, London, 1937, p. 21.

Modern Critics on Jane Austen

MARY LASCELLES: 1939

Jane Austen's Style

... What have been the character and direction of Jane Austen's development in that short course from *Sense and Sensibility* to *Persuasion*? For the present it will be enough to suggest that her consciousness has grown more subtle, her apprehension of her subject more complex; she has learnt to say what she has to say through her books, above all through the medium of her characters' consciousness; and (this is our immediate concern) she has formed a style fit for her purpose.

This development of style may be seen in its plainest aspect by finding out how it is that she can tell her story—how she makes exactly intelligible to us the symmetrically posed, precisely interrelated happenings that she chooses for narrative pattern—through the talk of her characters, even the most unpromising of them. A character of marked idiosyncrasies of speech, for example, does not seem well fitted to convey to the reader information of any complexity: one would not, as first sight, choose Miss Bates as the likeliest person to make clear to us so prettily complicated a comedy of errors as *Emma*. Yet this is her office. 'What is before me, I see,' she says (*Emma*, p. 176, chap. XXI), and she not only sees but conveys to us the exact circumstances at more than one turn of her niece's fortunes. Who would suppose that Miss Bates would be able to convey anything exactly? But, taking her time about it, she does—and that without using any mode of expression inconsistent with her usual habits of speech. Fanny Burney, faced with a like problem in *Camilla*, sacrifices consistency, and allows the muddle-headed Sir Hugh Tyrold to be more or less articulate as the plot requires; and it is not unusual to see a novelist slipping furtively round this obstacle with the words 'He related what had occurred'—and then giving his own account of the affair. But it is a consequence of Jane Austen's method that the obstacle itself should be much less formidable to her than it appears: look closely at the idiosyncrasies in speech of her characters, and they will show themselves to be modelled, as it were, in very low relief. This is how it comes about that Miss Bates's speech, while achieving an impression of inextricable confusion, is yet capable of making us understand the finest intricacies of the plot; that it forms a limpid element, in which its subject—her mother's spectacles, or the Perrys' carriage, or even the order of events at a crisis—is clearly apparent. This *limpid confusion* is the result of all its characteristics. First, she never misuses words (unless when she is recognizably quoting Mrs Elton); then, not one of her sentences can fairly be called confused; their structure and movement are as neat and brisk as her person. In fact, the impression of confusion is given by two habits which are so contrived as to counterbalance one another: in the first place, she seldom completes a sentence, though she usually carries it far enough to show how it should have been completed (a familiar English idiom): '. . . poor dear Jane could not bear to see anybody—anybody at all—Mrs Elton, indeed, could not be denied—and Mrs Cole had made such a point—and Mrs Perry had said so much—but, except them, Jane would really see nobody' (*Emma*, p. 390, chap. XLV). In the second place, each sentence flies off at a tangent from the last, but so characteristic are the trains of thought that, when need is, every sentence elucidates its curtailed predecessor—as a very small quotation will illustrate: '. . . upon my word, Miss Woodhouse, you do look —how do you like Jane's hair?' (*Emma*, p. 323, chap. XXXVIII). This use of fragmentary speech exacts more skill than does any other to which Jane Austen had turned it. She had employed it to suggest strong feeling, embarrassment—forces tugging against the impulse for expression—in Colonel Brandon's and Willoughby's accounts of themselves to Elinor, and was to use it for the same purpose in her first draft of Captain Wentworth's proposal of marriage. In such cases, its use is to alter the speaker's voice from its habitual tone—which in Willoughby's it had failed to do because we had not been allowed to hear enough of his ordinary voice. But for Miss Bates it *is* the habitual tone, and indicates not disorganization of the ordinary course of thought and feeling but that course itself. To represent a peculiar mode of progress requires greater delicacy of intimation than to represent arrest or disturbance of progress. And this delicacy of intimation is one consequence of that unemphatic treatment of idiosyncrasy which I have called low relief.

This same shallow modelling is discernible in all Jane Austen's dialogue. She tends to suggest social variants in speech by syntax and phrasing rather than by vocabulary, as appears when the elder, and less genteel, Miss Steele is compared with Fanny Burney's Branghtons; this is what Nancy makes of Edward's conversation with her sister, when she tries to report it to Elinor: '. . . it all came out . . . how he had been so worried by what passed, that as soon as he had went away from his mother's house, he had got upon his horse, and rid into the country some where or other; and how he had staid about at an inn all Thursday and Friday, on purpose to get the better of it.' And 'Edward have got some business at Oxford, he says; so he must go there for a time; and after *that*, as soon as he can light upon a Bishop, he will be ordained. I wonder what curacy he will get!' (*Sense and Sensibility*, pp. 273 and 275, chap. XXXVIII). This, though it is broad enough to embarrass her sister—who can manage the phrases of common talk pretty well, and is not likely to give herself away except in her letters—yet does not so differ in vocabulary from the speech of the Dashwoods as does that of the Branghtons from Evelina's. And it is syntax and phrasing likewise that differentiate the speech of the Thorpes from that of the Tilneys. Yet, in this shallow modelling, there is such exact keeping of scale that the distinctions remain clearly apparent: no sentence of Elizabeth Watson's could be transferred to her sister Emma, however their opinions may agree, because of their different upbringing; nor could a Steele vulgarism be mistaken for that of a Thorpe. Jane Austen never repeats herself. Each social shelf in her little world has its own slang— Isabella Thorpe's, Tom Bertram's, Mary Crawford's; and so have the professions, when they appear—Mr Shepherd's language has a recognizable flavour, though (to the relief, surely, of a generation that was becoming well acquainted with the lawyer of fiction) very sparingly used.

How did Jane Austen come by this mastery of dialogue? She must have had, to begin with, a fine and true ear.... Evidently she was an alert observer of mannerism in speech—at first, I suspect, because it irritated her; there is a note of exasperation in her treatment of Margaret Watson.[1] Later she learned how to draw its sting. Mannerism, especially when it takes the form of a recurrent word or phrase, is by no means easy to represent; there is but a hair's breadth between the point at which the reader delightedly recognizes it as a revealing habit of speech, and the point at which its iteration begins to weary him. But even as Mr Elton's 'Exactly so' is ready to catch the attention as an expression of his unfeeling complaisance, and before it can threaten tediousness, Emma transfixes it by her mimicry beyond the need of repetition: ' "This man is almost too gallant to be in love," thought Emma. "I should say so, but that I suppose there may be a hundred different ways of being in love. He is an excellent young man, and will suit Harriet exactly; it will be an 'Exactly so', as he says himself ..." ' (*Emma*, p. 49, chap. VI). Again, just as Miss Bates's idiom is beginning to tease the ear, Emma relieves pent feelings by her outrageous parody: she supposes Miss Bates to be thanking Mr

---

[1] '... her manner was all affection & her voice all gentleness; continual smiles & a very slow articulation being her constant resource when determined on pleasing.—She was now so "delighted to see dear, dear Emma" that she could hardly speak a word in a minute' (*The Watsons*, p. 87).

Knightley ' "for his great kindness in marrying Jane...—'So very kind and obliging!—But he always had been such a very kind neighbour!' And then fly off, through half a sentence, to her mother's old petticoat. 'Not that it was such a very old petticoat either—for still it would last a great while—and, indeed, she must thankfully say that their petticoats were all very strong.'" ' (*Emma*, p. 225, chap. XXVI). . .

[Jane Austen's characters have the ability to surprise us: to] . . . give us that tingling shock of the unexpected which will create the illusion of the living voice. This surprise must be delicately contrived, however, if it is not to blur the impression they have made on our imagination. And here again Jane Austen's use of 'low relief' proves its worth. For such relief can be momentarily heightened: a character may of a sudden—not casually, but under pressure of some sense of urgency—speak with deeper idiosyncrasy than usual. Such a pressure disturbs the habitual unaffected formality of Mr Woodhouse's speech when 'according to his custom on such occasions' he is 'making the circle of his guests, and paying his particular compliments to the ladies', last among them Jane Fairfax. For even as he generalizes, and allegorizes, and addresses her in the third person, momentarily, under the immediate pressure of his kindly solicitude, his voice alters in tone: 'I am very sorry to hear, Miss Fairfax, of your being out this morning in the rain. Young ladies should take care of themselves.— Young ladies are delicate plants. They should take care of their health and their complexion. My dear, did you change your stockings?' (*Emma*, p. 294, chap. XXXIV).

By what method did Jane Austen achieve this discreet use of idosyncrasy in speech? The corrections in her rough drafts seem to have something to tell. Both in *The Watsons* and in *Sanditon* she can be seen sketching out first what her characters have to communicate, and then marking, by gradual little touches, the manner of communication—as though a draftsman should first set a human figure in a certain attitude, and occupying a certain position in his composition, and then develop it into a particular figure, with proper characteristics of person and dress. In the opening of *The Watsons*, Emma and Elizabeth are introduced to us as they are driving together, 'in the old chair', 'to the town of D. in Surrey'; and the task of explaining the family's character and situation is given to Elizabeth, with the least possible help from the author's own voice. Now, looking into the corrections, one perceives that, while in the first draft Elizabeth simply tells what has to be told, this plain account is afterwards so modified by a number of minute touches—above all, by the substitution of little vulgarisms and colloquialisms for unaffected formal speech—as to indicate also the peculiar tone of the speaker. A reference to Tom Musgrave's habit of 'philandering' becomes: '. . . he is always behaving in a particular way to one or another' (*The Watsons*, p. 4, see Dr Chapman's note). Penelope's making 'no secret of wishing to marry' becomes: 'There is nothing she w^d not do to get married—she would as good as tell you so herself' (*The Watsons*, p. 6). And there is a steady and consistent substitution of short, plain words for longer synonyms throughout Elizabeth's speech. In *The Watsons*, it is true, Jane Austen seems to be struggling with a peculiar oppression, a stiffness and heaviness that threaten her style, and so the corrections show a general trend towards shorter, more colloquial words, in narrative as well as dialogue. But this does not hold good for *Sanditon*, nor does it sufficiently account for the systematic deepening, in the corrections of both manuscripts, of the idiosyncrasies in the speech of almost every character. Tom Musgrave's gallantry is a little broadened as he smirks at Emma in the assurance that he is making himself particularly agreeable: he has not, he easily admits, troubled to visit her family before her arrival: 'But I am afraid I have been a very sad neighbour of late. I hear dreadful complaints of my negligence wherever I go, & I confess it is a shameful length of time since I was at Stanton.—But I shall *now* endeavour to make myself amends for the past' (*The Watsons*, pp. 51, 52: 'I confess' and 'I shall *now* endeavour' are inserted in the revision). And a sharper edge is given to Mrs Watson's malice, a more sickly flavour to Margaret's affection, through such small changes. By the same means, of course, Jane Austen accentuates the amiable characteristics of her pleasant people: in recasting the end of *Persuasion* she uses some passages from the original draft, merely rewriting them; if one such passage—Wentworth's confession to Anne—is read in the two versions (*Two Chapters of Persuasion*, ed. Chapman, pp. 20, 21; *Persuasion*, pp. 242, 243, chap. XXIII), it will be found that, by little corrections in the first, and little alterations when she comes to make the second, she has heightened the vehemence and candour with which he blames himself for his pride and obstinacy. The corrections in the manuscript of *Sanditon* show this same gradual differentiation in the speech of the several characters: Mr Parker's idiom, his habit of thinking *in phrases*, becomes more marked; the relation of her past history by Lady Denham to Charlotte acquires her peculiar intonation through vulgarisms in syntax: 'We lived perfectly happily together' becomes 'Nobody could live happier together than us' (*Sanditon*, p. 97); and a little button of absurdity is fastened on top of Sir Edward's pretentious vocabulary by the substitution of 'anti-puerile' for 'sagacious' in his description of the ideal novel-reader—that is, of himself (*Sanditon*, p. 108).

'I hate re-writing,' Scott said, 'as much as Falstaff did paying back' (*Chronicles of the Canongate*, chap. V). I should not be surprised to learn that Jane Austen positively enjoyed it.

This style, with its quick and light response to idiosyncrasy, allows Jane Austen's characters to be, so far as we are concerned, *communicative*—and that in a natural and probable manner. Their faculty of

observation varies, of course; nicety of perception belongs only to her
favourites; but they can all tell us something about one another. 'I do
not think Mr Knightley would be much disturbed by Miss Bates,'
Mrs Weston says. 'Little things do not irritate him. She might talk on;
and if he wanted to say any thing himself, he would only talk louder,
and drown her voice' (*Emma*, pp. 225, 226, chap. XXVI). Yet these
communications never appear to come from the author's own fund of
knowledge, because they so faithfully observe the idiom of the
character through whom they reach us, whether in the form of dialogue,
letter, or reflection. Few novelists can be more scrupulous than Jane
Austen as to the phrasing of the thoughts of their characters. Mr
Bennet, believing that his brother-in-law had borne the cost of Lydia's
marriage, wished that he had made provision for his daughters: 'Had
he done his duty in that respect, Lydia need not have been indebted
to her uncle, for whatever of honour or credit could now be purchased
for her. The satisfaction of prevailing on one of the most worthless
young men in Great Britain to be her husband, might then have rested
in its proper place' (*Pride and Prejudice*, p. 308, chap. L). His letters
are equally characteristic, and, like all the letters in Jane Austen's
novels, nicely differentiated from the speech of the writer. The men's
letters always show a very little increase of formality, which sharpens
the point of Mr Bennet's wit, lends weight to Darcy's assertions, and
elaborates Frank Churchill's compliments; the women seldom attempt
this formality, unless, like Lucy Steele, they are straining after
gentility; nevertheless, a passage from one of their letters could rarely
be mistaken for a passage of dialogue, since these letters catch and
hold a mood as speech can rarely do—Lydia's exhilaration in eloping,
Jane's distress and confusion in telling Elizabeth of the elopement. It
may be worth noticing here than Jane Austen had no very useful model
for her fictitious letters. The novel-in-letters, being obliged to relieve
the density of narrative by dialogue, formed a convention which only
this need could justify: the convention of long conversations reported
word for word. The letters of stage-comedy were not subject to this
convention, but they must be concise and crucial. Neither offered a
precedent for the lifelikeness of Mary Musgrove's letter, with its
transplantation of others' talk into her own idiom, and its news in the
postscript.

The virtue of this style which Jane Austen has made to be the
means of communication of her characters lies in its equitable settle-
ment of conflicting claims; not only does it allow her people to be
constant without becoming static, but it gives them a language in
which they may speak to us as they would while telling us what she
means that they should. Moreover it achieves harmony with her
narrative manner. . . . Jane Austen's narrative style seems to me to
show (especially in the later novels) a curiously chameleon-like faculty;
it varies in colour as the habits of expression of the several characters

impress themselves on the relation of the episodes in which they are involved, and on the description of their situations. The very arrival of the Bertrams' party in the midst of the solemn grandeur of Sotherton seems to weigh it down:

> 'Mr Rushworth was at the door to receive his fair lady, and the whole party were welcomed by him with due attention. In the drawing-room they were met with equal cordiality by the mother, and Miss Bertram had all the distinction with each that she could wish. After the business of arriving was over, it was first necessary to eat, and the doors were thrown open to admit them through one or two intermediate rooms into the appointed dining-parlour, where a collation was prepared with abundance and elegance' (*Mansfield Park*, p. 84, chap. IX).

As they make their progress through the house, with its 'solid mahogany, rich damask, marble, gilding and carving', this abundance and elegance seem to lie like an increasing load upon the imagination, until, half stupefied with the air of Sotherton, we reach the appropriate anti-climax of Mrs Rushworth's 'relation': 'This chapel was fitted up as you see it, in James the Second's time. Before that period, as I understand, the pews were only wainscot; and there is some reason to think that the linings and cushions of the pulpit and family-seat were only purple cloth; but this is not quite certain' (*Mansfield Park*, p. 86, chap. IX).

This aptitude that I have likened to a chameleon's is, however, no more than a symptom of the pliability of Jane Austen's narrative style; and that pliability is due to the essential simplicity of its staple. Here she was fortunate and judicious; she inherited a good tradition, and she was content with it. As for prose, her brother tells us that 'Her reading was very extensive in history and *belles lettres*; and her memory extremely tenacious'; that she was acquainted with 'the best essays and novels in the English language'; and among the graver writings he singles out Johnson's (*Biographical Notice*, 1817, p. xv). She was brought up, in fact, on the standard authors of her own and the preceding age, and their habits of thought and expression might become hers, if she were so disposed.

She did not look to the novelists for direction as to style; and this was well, for the great novels of the mid-eighteenth century had too strong individuality, and their successor, the novel of sentiment, did not know its own business. It wanted, not merely a grand style for its more ambitious passages, but also an unaffected, level style for plain relation of fact and circumstance. . . .

Jane Austen and Her Art, Oxford, 1939, pp. 93–103. The substance of the section on style was published earlier in 'Some Characteristics of Jane Austen's Style', *Essays and Studies*, Vol. XXII, 1937, pp. 61–85. The page references are to R. W. Chapman's edition of the novels.

Regulated Hatred: An Aspect of the Work of Jane Austen

The impression of Jane Austen which has filtered through to the reading public down from the first-hand critics, through histories of literature, university courses, literary journalism and polite allusion, deters many who might be her best readers from bothering with her at all. How can this popular impression be described? In my experience the first idea to be absorbed from the atmosphere surrounding her work was that she offered exceptionally favourable openings to the exponents of urbanity. Gentlemen of an older generation than mine spoke of their intention of re-reading her on their deathbeds; Eric Linklater's cultured Prime Minister in *The Impregnable Women* passes from surreptitious to abandoned reading of her novels as a national crisis deepens. With this there also came the impression that she provided a refuge for the sensitive when the contemporary world grew too much for them. So Beatrice Kean Seymour writes (*Jane Austen*): 'In a society which has enthroned the machine-gun and carried it aloft even into the quiet heavens, there will always be men and women—Escapist or not, as you please—who will turn to her novels with an unending sense of relief and thankfulness.'

I was given to understand that her scope was of course extremely restricted, but that within her limits she succeeded admirably in expressing the gentler virtues of a civilized social order. She could do this because she lived at a time when, as a sensitive person of culture, she could still feel that she had a place in society and could address the reading public as sympathetic equals; she might introduce unpleasant people into her stories but she could confidently expose them to a public opinion that condemned them. Chiefly, so I gathered, she was a delicate satirist, revealing with inimitable lightness of touch the comic foibles and amiable weaknesses of the people whom she lived amongst and liked.

All this was enough to make me quite certain I didn't want to read her. And it is, I believe, a seriously misleading impression. Fragments of the truth have been incorporated in it but they are fitted into a pattern whose total effect is false. And yet the wide currency of this false impression is an indication of Jane Austen's success in an essential part of her complex intention as a writer: her books are, as she meant them to be, read and enjoyed by precisely the sort of people whom she disliked; she is a literary classic of the society which attitudes like hers, held widely enough, would undermine.

In order to enjoy her books without disturbance those who retain the conventional notion of her work must always have had slightly to misread what she wrote at a number of scattered points, points where she took good care (not wittingly perhaps) that the misreading should be the easiest thing in the world. Unexpected astringencies occur which the comfortable reader probably overlooks, or else passes by as slight imperfections, trifling errors of tone brought about by a faulty choice of words. Look at the passage in *Northanger Abbey* where Henry Tilney offers a solemn reprimand of Catherine's fantastic suspicions about his father:

> 'Dear Miss Morland, consider the dreadful nature of these suspicions you have entertained. What have you been judging from? Remember the country and the age in which we live. Remember that we are English, that we are Christians. Consult your own understanding, your own sense of the probable, your own observation of what is passing around you. Does our education prepare us for such atrocities? Do our laws connive at them? Could they be perpetrated without being known, in a country like this, where social and literary intercourse is on such a footing, and where roads and newspapers lay everything open?'

Had the passage really been as I quote it nothing would have been out of tone. But I omitted a clause. The last sentence actually runs: 'Could they be perpetrated without being known, in a country like this, where social and literary intercourse is on such a footing, where every man is surrounded by a neighbourhood of voluntary spies, and where roads and newspapers lay everything open?' 'Where every man is surrounded by a neighbourhood of voluntary spies'—with its touch of paranoia that surprising remark is badly out of tune both with 'Henry's astonishing generosity and nobleness of conduct' and with the accepted idea of Jane Austen.

Yet it comes quite understandably from someone of Jane Austen's sensitive intelligence, living in her world of news and gossip interchanged amongst and around a large family. She writes to Cassandra (September 14, 1804), 'My mother is at this moment reading a letter from my aunt. Yours to Miss Irvine of which she had had the perusal (which by the bye in your place I should not like) has thrown them into a quandary about Charles and his prospects. The case is that my mother had previously told my aunt, without restriction, that . . . whereas you had replied to Miss Irvine's inquiries on the subject with less explicitness and more caution. Never mind, let them puzzle on together.' And when Fanny Knight (her niece) writes confidentially about her love affair, Jane Austen describes ruses she adopted to avoid having to read the letter to the family, and later implores Fanny to 'write *something* that may do to be read or told' (November 30, 1814).

Why is it that, holding the view she did of people's spying, Jane Austen should slip it in amongst Henry Tilney's eulogies of the age? By doing so she achieves two ends, ends which she may not have consciously aimed at. In such a speech from such a character the remark is unexpected and unbelievable, with the result that it is quite unlikely to be taken in at all by many readers; it slips through their minds without creating a disturbance. It gets said, but with the minimum risk of setting people's backs up. The second end achieved by giving the remark such a context is that of off-setting it at once by more appreciative views of society and so refraining from indulging an exaggerated bitterness. The eulogy of the age is not nullified by the bitter clause, but neither can it wipe out the impression the clause makes on those who attend to it.

One cannot say that here the two attitudes modify one another. The technique is too weak. Jane Austen can bring both attitudes into the picture but she has not at this point made one picture of them. In *Persuasion* she does something of the same kind more delicately. Miss Elliot's chagrin at having failed to marry her cousin is being described in the terms of ordinary satire which invites the reading public to feel superior to Miss Elliot:

> There was not a baronet from A to Z whom her feelings could have so willingly acknowledged as an equal. Yet so miserably had he conducted himself, that though she was at this present time (the summer of 1814) wearing black ribbons for his wife, she could not admit him to be worth thinking of again. The disgrace of his first marriage might, perhaps, as there was no reason to suppose it perpetuated by offspring, have been got over, had he not done worse;

—and then at this point the satire suddenly directs itself against the public instead of Miss Elliot—

> but he had, as by the accustomary intervention of kind friends they had been informed, spoken most disrespectfully of them all. . . .

In *Emma* the same thing is done still more effectively. Again Jane Austen seems to be on perfectly good terms with the public she is addressing and to have no reserve in offering the funniness and virtues of Mr Woodhouse and Miss Bates to be judged by the accepted standards of the public. She invites her readers to be just their natural patronizing selves. But this public that Jane Austen seems on such good terms with has some curious things said about it, not criticisms, but small notes of fact that are usually not made. They almost certainly go unnoticed by many readers, for they involve only the faintest change of tone from something much more usual and acceptable.

When she says that Miss Bates 'enjoyed a most uncommon degree of popularity for a woman neither young, handsome, rich nor married', this is fairly conventional satire that any reading public would cheerfully admit in its satirist and chuckle over. But the next sentence must have to be mentally re-written by the greater number of Jane Austen's readers. For them it probably runs, 'Miss Bates stood in the very worst predicament in the world for having much of the public favour; and she had no intellectual superiority to make atonement to herself, or compel an outward respect from those who might despise her.' This, I suggest, is how most readers, lulled and disarmed by the amiable context, will soften what in fact reads, '. . . and she had no intellectual superiority to make atonement to herself, or frighten those who might hate her into outward respect.' Jane Austen was herself at this time 'neither young, handsome, rich, nor married', and the passage perhaps hints at the functions which her unquestioned intellectual superiority may have had for her.

This eruption of fear and hatred into the relationships of everyday social life is something that the urbane admirer of Jane Austen finds distasteful; it is not the satire of one who writes securely for the entertainment of her civilized acquaintances. And it has the effect, for the attentive reader, of changing the flavour of the more ordinary satire amongst which it is embedded.

Emma is especially interesting from this point of view. What is sometimes called its greater 'mellowness' largely consists in saying quietly and undisguisedly things which in the earlier books were put more loudly but in the innocuous form of caricature. Take conversation for instance. Its importance and its high (though by no means supreme) social value are of course implicit in Jane Austen's writings. But one should beware of supposing that a mind like hers therefore found the ordinary social intercourse of the period congenial and satisfying. In *Pride and Prejudice* she offers an entertaining caricature of card-table conversation at Lady Catherine de Bourgh's house.

> Their table was superlatively stupid. Scarcely a syllable was uttered that did not relate to the game, except when Mrs Jenkinson expressed her fears of Miss de Bourgh's being too hot or too cold, or having too much or too little light. A great deal more passed at the other table. Lady Catherine was generally speaking—stating the mistakes of the three others, or relating some anecdote of herself. Mr Collins was employed in agreeing to everything her ladyship said, thanking her for every fish he won, and apologizing if he thought he won too many. Sir William did not say much. He was storing his memory with anecdotes and noble names.

This invites the carefree enjoyment of all her readers. They can all feel superior to Lady Catherine and Mr Collins. But in *Emma* the style changes: the talk at the Cole's dinner party, a pleasant dinner party which the heroine enjoyed, is described as '. . . the usual rate of conversation; a few clever things said, a few downright silly, but by much the larger proportion neither the one nor the other—nothing worse than everyday remarks, dull repetitions, old news, and heavy jokes.' 'Nothing worse'!—that phrase is typical. It is not mere sarcasm by any means. Jane Austen genuinely valued the achievements of the civilization she lived within and never lost sight of the fact that there might be something vastly worse than the conversation she referred to. 'Nothing worse' is a positive tribute to the decency, the superficial friendliness, the absence of the grosser forms of insolence and self-display at the dinner party. At least Mrs Elton wasn't there. And yet the effect of the comment, if her readers took it seriously, would be that of a disintegrating attack upon the sort of social intercourse they have established for themselves. It is not the comment of one who would have helped to make her society what it was, or ours what it is.

To speak of this aspect of her work as 'satire' is perhaps misleading. She has none of the underlying didactic intention ordinarily attributed to the satirist. Her object is not missionary; it is the more desperate one of merely finding some mode of existence for her critical attitudes. To her the first necessity was to keep on reasonably good terms with the associates of her everyday life; she had a deep need of their affection and a genuine respect for the ordered, decent civilization that they upheld. And yet she was sensitive to their crudenesses and complacencies and knew that her real existence depended on resisting many of the values they implied. The novels gave her a way out of this dilemma. This, rather than the ambition of entertaining a posterity of urbane gentlemen, was her motive force in writing.

As a novelist, therefore, part of her aim was to find the means for unobtrusive spiritual survival, without open conflict with the friendly people around her whose standards in simpler things she could accept and whose affection she greatly needed. She found, of course, that one of the most useful peculiarities of her society was its willingness to remain blind to the implications of a caricature. She found people eager to laugh at faults they tolerated in themselves and their friends, so long as the faults were exaggerated and the laughter 'good-natured'— so long, that is, as the assault on society could be regarded as a mock assault and not genuinely disruptive. Satire such as this is obviously a means not of admonition but of self-preservation.

Hence one of Jane Austen's most successful methods is to offer her readers every excuse for regarding as rather exaggerated figures of fun people whom she herself detests and fears. Mrs Bennet, according to the Austen tradition, is one of 'our' richly comic characters about whom we can feel superior, condescending, perhaps a trifle sympathetic, and above all heartily amused and free from care. Everything conspires to make this the natural interpretation once you are willing to overlook Jane Austen's bald and brief statement of her own attitude to her: 'She was a woman of mean understanding, little information, and uncertain temper.' How many women amongst Jane Austen's acquaintance and amongst her most complacent readers to the present day that phrase must describe! How gladly they enjoy the funny side of the situations Mrs Bennet's unpleasant nature creates, and how easy it is made for them to forget or never observe that Jane Austen, none the less for seeing how funny she is, goes on detesting her. The thesis that the ruling standards of our social group leave a perfectly comfortable niche for detestable people and give them sufficient sanction to persist, would, if it were argued seriously, arouse the most violent opposition, the most determined apologetics for things as they are, and the most reproachful pleas for a sense of proportion.

Caricature served Jane Austen's purpose perfectly. Under her treatment one can never say where caricature leaves off and the claim to serious portraiture begins. Mr Collins is only given a trifle more comic exaggeration than Lady Catherine de Bourgh, and by her standards is a possible human being. Lady Catherine in turn seems acceptable as a portrait if the criterion of verisimilitude is her nephew Mr Darcy. And he, finally, although to some extent a caricature, is near enough natural portraiture to stand beside Elizabeth Bennet, who, like all the heroines, is presented as an undistorted portrait. The simplest comic effects are gained by bringing the caricatures into direct contact with the real people, as in Mr Collins' visit to the Bennets and his proposal to Elizabeth. But at the same time one knows that, though from some points of view a caricature, in other directions he does, by easy stages, fit into the real world. He is real enough to Mrs Bennet; and she is real enough to Elizabeth to create a situation of real misery for her when she refuses. Consequently the proposal scene is not only comic fantasy, but it is also, for Elizabeth, a taste of the fantastic nightmare in which economic and social institutions have such power over the values of personal relationships that the comic monster is nearly able to get her.

The implications of her caricatures as criticism of real people in real society is brought out in the way they dovetail into their social setting. The decent, stodgy Charlotte puts up cheerfully with Mr Collins as a husband; and Elizabeth can never quite become reconciled to the idea that her friend is the wife of her comic monster. And that, of course, is precisely the sort of idea that Jane Austen herself could never grow reconciled to. The people she hated were tolerated, accepted, comfortably ensconced in the only human society she knew; they were, for her, society's embarrassing unconscious comment on itself. A recent writer on Jane Austen, Elizabeth Jenkins, puts forward the polite and more comfortable interpretation in supposing Charlotte's marriage to be explained solely by the impossibility of young women's earning their own living at that period. But Charlotte's complaisance goes deeper than that: it is shown as a considered indifference to personal relationships when they conflict with cruder advantages in the wider social world:

> She had always felt that Charlotte's opinion of matrimony was not exactly like her own, but she could not have supposed it possible that, when called into action, she would have sacrificed every better feeling to worldly advantage.

We know too, at the biographical level, that Jane Austen herself, in a precisely similar situation to Charlotte's, spent a night of psychological crisis in deciding to revoke her acceptance of an 'advantageous' proposal made the previous evening. And her letters to Fanny Knight show how deep her convictions went at this point.

It is important to notice that Elizabeth makes no break with her friend on account of the marriage. This was the sort of friend—'a friend disgracing herself and sunk in her esteem'—that went to make up the available social world which one could neither escape materially nor be independent of psychologically. The impossibility of being cut off from objectionable people is suggested more subtly in *Emma,* where Mrs Elton is the highlight of the pervasive neglect of spiritual values in social life. One can hardly doubt that Jane Austen's own dealings with society are reflected in the passage where Mr Weston makes the error of inviting Mrs Elton to joint the picnic party which he and Emma have planned:

> ... Emma could not but feel some surprise, and a little displeasure, on hearing from Mr Weston that he had been proposing to Mrs Elton, as her brother and sister had failed her, that the two parties should unite, and go together, and that as Mrs Elton had very readily acceded to it, so it was to be, if she had no objection. Now, as her objection was nothing but her very great dislike of Mrs Elton, of which Mr Weston must already be perfectly aware, it was not worth bringing forward: it could not be done without a reproof to him, which would be giving pain to his wife; and she found herself, therefore, obliged to consent to an arrangement which she would have done a great deal to avoid; an arrangement which would, probably, expose her even to the degradation of being said to be of Mrs Elton's party! Every feeling was offended, and the forbearance of her outward submission left a heavy arrear due of secret severity in her reflections, on the unmanageable good-will of Mr Weston's temper.
>
> 'I am glad you approve of what I have done,' said he, very comfortably. 'But I thought you would. Such schemes as these are nothing without numbers. One cannot have too large a party. A large party secures its own amusement. And she is a good-natured woman after all. One could not leave her out.'

Emma denied none of it aloud, and agreed to none of it in private.

This well illustrates Jane Austen's typical dilemma: of being intensely critical of people to whom she also has strong emotional attachments. . . .

Scrutiny, Vol. VIII, March 1940, pp. 346–55 (346–62). This article was originally a paper read to the Literary Society of Manchester University, March 3, 1939.

The Economic Determination of Jane Austen

... Jane Austen's social and psychological environment was ... that of the eighteenth-century country gentleman. The industrial revolution and nineteenth-century capitalism had not impinged upon it or upon her, and not a breath from them ruffles the surface of her novels. Whatever determined her economically was not the Victorian type of capitalism which left such clear marks on the novels of Dickens and Thackeray. That is why I find it surprising that her social and economic standards should be, except in one important particular, those which we associate with a capitalist bourgeoisie rather than with country gentlemen and aristocrats....

I will begin ... with the exception ... Jane's attitude to 'work' is the antithesis of that of a capitalist, and pre-eminently of the Victorian bourgeoisie. There is hardly a single male character in her novels who does any work; to work at all is, indeeed, almost incompatible with the status of a gentleman. She recognizes as socially possible only the following professions: the army and navy, the Church, and, with some reservations, the law. Of these professions only the army and navy are usually considered to be unobjectionable. Even so, it will be remembered, Anne Elliot was prevented by her family from marrying Captain Wentworth, because her father 'thought it a very degrading alliance'. 'The profession,' says Sir Walter Elliot, 'has its utility, but I should be sorry to see any friend of mine belonging to it'; and his reasons are two, the profession is offensive, 'first, as being the means of bringing persons of obscure birth into undue distinction', and second, because sailors 'are all knocked about and exposed to every climate, and every weather, till they are not fit to be seen'. 'A man,' he sums up, 'is in greater danger in the navy of being insulted by the rise of one whose father, his father might have disdained to speak to, and of becoming prematurely an object of disgust himself, than in any other line.' In applying the Marxian dialectic to Jane Austen, one must, of course, always remember that she is one of the greatest and subtlest of satirists, and the remark of Sir Walter Elliot, of Kellynch Hall, must not be treated quite as seriously as 'facts' are dealt with—sometimes perhaps with equally small reason—by Marxists. But if Jane's smile hovers over Sir Walter, Lady Russell, who is represented as an unusually sensible woman, supported him in preventing the match, and the mature

Anne, who had lived to regret having been persuaded by Lady Russell, still admitted her prudence.

As a profession, the navy is regarded by Jane Austen and her characters almost exclusively as a means to obtaining either a position or money. No other profession receives any consideration but the Church and the law. She knew that a gentleman might be a lawyer, but she hardly takes the profession seriously. . . .

Out of six heroes three are clergymen or prospective clergymen. But none of them seem to *work* as clergymen. . . . This attitude towards 'work', profession and trade is, I suppose, characteristic of a landed aristocracy or gentry. Otherwise the economic determination of Jane Austen is of the type which one usually associates with a capitalistic bourgeoisie. The social standards are almost entirely those of money and snobbery. It is remarkable to what an extent the plots and characters are dominated by questions of money. . . . The axis of the plot in every novel except *Emma* is money and marriage or rank and marriage. The social standard, ideal, and duty of a woman is assumed to be to marry as high or as rich as possible, and we know, on Mrs Bennet's evidence that, according to the tariff, £10,000 a year was as good as a lord. . . .

The only social standard in the novels which competes with money is snobbery. It is true that this snobbery is a favourite subject of Jane Austen's satire but Lady Catherine de Bourgh and Sir Walter Elliot are only ridiculous in being exaggerated. All the characters are fundamentally snobs with regard to class, and their snobbery is the same as that of the Victorian bourgeoisie. Every one of the novels ends happily and the end is happy in four out of the six because the heroine, in spite of difficulties, marries above herself. *Emma*, it is true, does not marry above herself, but she is the most snobbish of all the heroines. She can tell Harriet that she (Emma) could not have visited her (Harriet) if she had married the yeoman, Robert Martin— 'you would have thrown yourself out of all good society'. And the reason she gives illuminates the class consciousness of Jane Austen's environment:

'The yeomanry are precisely the order of people with whom I feel I can have nothing to do. A degree or two lower, and a creditable appearance might interest me; I might hope to be useful to their families in some way or other. But a farmer can need none of my help, and is, therefore, in one sense, as much above my notice, as in every other he is below it.'

It sounds like the Charity Organization Society in the eighteen-nineties.

New Statesman and Nation, n.s. Vol. XXIV, July 18, 1942, pp. 40–1 (39–41).

The Controlling Hand: Jane Austen and *Pride and Prejudice*

The remarkable thing in *Pride and Prejudice* as in the other novels of Jane Austen is the mind of Jane Austen. If it could be proved—and Mrs Leavis has shown (Q. D. Leavis, 'A Critical Theory of Jane Austen's Writings: III, The Letters'; *Scrutiny*, Vol XII, Spring, 1944) very clearly that it cannot—that the 'real' Jane Austen who lived in Chawton was, as Mr Forster ruefully suggests, a person of rather trivial intelligence and crude manners, the proof would be irrelevant to our reading of the novels. For as literary critics we are concerned only with the mind that appears in the novels and which we can reconstruct from their language. What is distinctive about this mind is its control: the union of alertness of the many possible meanings of a human action with the steady power of making precisely defined statements of this ambiguity.

In *Pride and Prejudice,* particularly in the presentation of Darcy's character, Jane Austen shows an almost Jamesian awareness of the multiple ways of reading a man's behaviour. She conveys her sense of the possibility of very different interpretations of the 'same' action, as James often does, through dialogues which look trivial and which are extremely ambiguous. At the same time they are not merely confusing because Jane Austen defines so precisely the ironic implications of what is said and because she gradually limits the possibilities with which the reader is to be most concerned. So the book moves toward the 'more reasonable' interpretation at the climax, in which Elizabeth readjusts her whole view of her lover. There is in passing ambiguity aplenty, as anyone can see by looking over the earlier conversations between Elizabeth and Darcy. But as the reader goes on, he sees that he has been prepared for the climax by a skilful allowance for alternative 'readings' of Darcy's character, and he realizes that limits have been set on the relevant possibilities. By analysis of a few of these 'trivial' dialogues we shall see that both the range and the definition of ironic implications are realized through a finely controlled use of words.

What most satisfies a present-day reader in following the central drama is Jane Austen's awareness that it is difficult to 'know' any complex person, that knowledge of a man like Darcy is an interpretation and a construction, not a simple absolute. Like the characters of Proust, the chief persons in *Pride and Prejudice* are not the same when projected through the conversation of different people. The *snobisme* of Darcy's talk, like Swann's, changes according to the group he is with. Mr Darcy is hardly recognizable as the 'same' man when he is described by Mr Wickham, or his housekeeper, or Elizabeth, or Mr Bingley.

It is the complex persons, the 'intricate characters', that require and merit interpretation as Elizabeth points out in the pleasant conversation in which she tells Bingley that she 'understands him perfectly':

> 'You begin to comprehend me, do you?' cried he, turning towards her.
>
> 'Oh! Yes—I understand you perfectly.'
>
> 'I wish I might take this for a compliment; but to be so easily seen through I am afraid is pitiful.'
>
> 'That is as it happens. It does not necessarily follow that a deep, intricate character is more or less estimable than such a one as yours.'
>
> 'Lizzy,' cried her mother, 'remember where you are, and do not run on in the wild manner that you are suffered to do at home.'
>
> 'I did not know before,' continued Bingley immediately, 'that you were a studier of character. It must be an amusing study.'
>
> 'Yes; but intricate characters are the *most* amusing. They have at least that advantage.'
>
> 'The country,' said Darcy, 'can in general supply but few subjects for such a study. In a country neighbourhood you move in a very confined and unvarying society.'
>
> 'But people themselves alter so much, that there is something new to be observed for ever.'

Elizabeth's remark with its ironic application to Darcy indicates the interest which makes the book 'go' and shows the type of awareness we are analyzing. 'Intricate characters are the *most* amusing', because their behaviour can be taken in so many ways, because they are not always the same people. The man we know today is a different man tomorrow. Naturally, we infer, people will not be equally puzzling to every judge. Mr Bingley and Jane find Mr Darcy a much less 'teazing man' than Elizabeth does. It is only the Elizabeths, the adult minds, who will 'observe something new' in the 'same old' people.

The subtlety of this awareness of 'intricacy' and the way in which is is dramatically realized are nicely shown in the dialogue just quoted. As elsewhere in Jane Austen there is an irony beyond the immediate irony, a smile beyond the first smile. In the context of Elizabeth's later discoveries and of her naïve trust of Wickham, it is delightful to hear her assume that she is 'a studier of character'. There is a shade of aptness in Mrs Bennet's silly rebuke.

The aura of implications which surrounds these early dialogues between Elizabeth and Darcy is complex enough to delight the most pure Empsonian. Take for example the dialogue in which Sir William Lucas attempts to interest Mr Darcy in dancing:

> ... Elizabeth at that instant moving towards them, he was struck with the notion of doing a very gallant thing, and called out to her,
> 'My dear Miss Eliza, why are not you dancing?—Mr Darcy, you must allow me to present this young lady to you as a very desirable partner—You cannot refuse to dance, I am sure, when so much beauty is before you.' And taking her hand, he would have given it to Mr Darcy, who, though extremely surprised, was not unwilling to receive it, when she instantly drew back, and said with some discomposure to Sir William,
> 'Indeed, Sir, I have not the least intention of dancing—I entreat you not to suppose that I moved this way in order to beg a partner.'
> Mr Darcy with grave propriety requested to be allowed the honour of her hand; but in vain. Elizabeth was determined; nor did Sir William at all shake her purpose by his attempt at persuasion.
> 'You excel so much in the dance, Miss Eliza, that it is cruel to deny me the happiness of seeing you; and though this gentleman dislikes the amusement in general, he can have no objection, I am sure, to oblige us for one half hour.'
> 'Mr Darcy is all politeness,' said Elizabeth, smiling.
> 'He is indeed—but considering the inducement, my dear Eliza, we cannot wonder at his complaisance; for who would object to such a partner?'
> Elizabeth looked archly, and turned away.

'Mr Darcy is all politeness': the statement, as Elizabeth might say, has a 'reazing' variety of meanings. Mr Darcy is polite in the sense indicated by 'grave propriety', that is, he shows the civility appropriate to a gentleman—which is the immediate, public meaning of Elizabeth's compliment. But 'grave propriety', being a very limited form of politeness, reminds us forcibly of Mr Darcy's earlier behaviour. His 'gravity' at the ball had been 'forbidding and disagreeable'. 'Grave propriety' may also mean the bare civility of 'the proudest, most disagreeable man in the world'. So Elizabeth's compliment has an ironic twist: she smiles and looks 'archly'. 'All politeness' has also quite another meaning. Mr Darcy 'was not unwilling to receive' her hand. He is polite in more than the public proper sense; his gesture shows that he is interested in Elizabeth as a person. So her archness and her smile have for the reader an added ironic value: Elizabeth's interpretation of Darcy's manner may be quite wrong. Finally there is the embracing broadly comic irony of Sir William's action. 'Struck with the notion of doing a very gallant thing', he is pleasantly unconscious

of what he is in fact doing and of what Elizabeth's remark may mean
to her and to Darcy.

There is a similar cluster of possibilities in another conversation
in which Darcy asks Elizabeth to dance with him:

> ... soon afterwards Mr Darcy, drawing near Elizabeth, said to
> her—
>
> 'Do not you feel a great inclination, Miss Bennet, to seize such
> an opportunity of dancing a reel?'
>
> She smiled, but made no answer. He repeated the question, with
> some surprise at her silence.
>
> 'Oh!' said she, 'I heard you before; but I could not immediately
> determine what to say in reply. You wanted me, I know, to say
> "Yes", that you might have the pleasure of despising my taste;
> but I always delight in overthrowing those kind of schemes, and
> cheating a person of their premeditated contempt. I have therefore
> made up my mind to tell you, that I do not want to dance a reel
> at all—and now despise me if you dare.'
>
> 'Indeed I do not dare.'
>
> Elizabeth, having rather expected to affront him, was amazed
> at his gallantry; but there was a mixture of sweetness and archness
> in her manner which made it difficult for her to affront anybody; and
> Darcy had never been so bewitched by any woman as he was by her.
> He really believed, that were it not for the inferiority of her
> connections, he should be in some danger.
>
> Miss Bingley saw, or suspected enough to be jealous; and her
> great anxiety for the recovery of her dear friend Jane, received
> some assistance from her desire of getting rid of Elizabeth.
>
> She often tried to provoke Darcy into disliking her guest, by
> talking of their supposed marriage, and planning his happiness in
> such an alliance.

We can find considerable 'amusement' in exploring the various tones
of voice appropriate for reading Mr Darcy's speeches. Elizabeth hears
his question as expressing 'premeditated contempt' and scorn of her
own taste. But from Mr Darcy's next remark and the comment which
follows it and from his repeating his question and showing 'some
surprise', we may hear in his request a tone expressive of some interest,
perhaps only gallantry, perhaps, as Elizabeth later puts it, 'somewhat
of a friendlier nature'. We could hear his 'Indeed I do not dare' as
pure gallantry (Elizabeth's version) or as a sign of conventional
'marriage intentions' (Miss Bingley's interpretation), if it were not for
the nice reservation, 'He really believed, that were it not for the
inferiority of her connections, he should be in some danger'. We must
hear the remark in a tone which includes this qualification. This
simultaneity of tonal 'layers' can be matched only in the satire of
Pope, where again a sensitive reader will feel the impossibility of

adjusting his voice to the rapidity of change in tone and the difficulty of representing by a single sound the several sounds he hears as equally appropriate and necessary. Analysis such as I have been making shows very clearly how arbitrary and how thin any stage rendering of *Pride and Prejudice* must be. No speaking voice could possibly represent the variety of tones which is conveyed to the reader by such interplay of dialogue and comment. For once a comparison with music may not be misleading. Reading Jane Austen may be rightly compared to hearing a Mozart opera, where the music, especially the orchestration, serves as a contrasting and enriching commentary (witty or serious) on the words of arias and recitatives and on the dramatic situation. . . .

But these conversations are not simply 'sets of ironic meanings'; they are, in more than the trivial sense, *jeux d'esprit*, the play of an adult mind. The sophistication they imply is of a kind which, as John Jay Chapman once suggested, is Greek and French, rather than English. The fun in Jane Austen's dialogue has a serious point; or rather, the fun *is* the point. The small talk is the focus for her keen sense of the variability of 'character', for her awareness of the possibility that the 'same' remark or action has very different meanings in different relations. And the ordered range of ironies is the proof of her immense literary power, of her ability to compel language to express this peculiar awareness.

We can see this control more clearly in the management of the dialogue in relation to the main sequence of *Pride and Prejudice*. By finely graduated steps we are led to form a new estimate of Darcy's character, a revision which is prepared for in part by the slow revelation of his altering attitude to Elizabeth. The refinement in this progress is, especially by modern standards, rather wonderful. Perhaps the best example is the scene in which one of the main signs of a change is Mr Darcy's twice moving his chair. Through scenes of similar refinement the dialogue is delicately shaped toward Elizabeth's recognition that Darcy regards her differently and that she has herself suffered a 'change of sentiment' toward him. Though the sense of a rich texture of amusement is never lost, attention is being constantly directed toward the main alternative judgments of Darcy.

The main choices are defined for the reader in various ways. There is first the underlying reference to the symbolic abstractions of Pride and Prejudice. Naturally it would be, in Elizabeth's phrase, 'superlatively stupid' to read the novel as a set of illustrations of these or other Moral Passions. Only a few of the cruder scenes of the book approach this level: the more obvious of Miss Bingley's exhibitions of snobbery, Lady Catherine quizzing Elizabeth on the upbringing of her sisters, or Mr Collins making his proposal—which might be labelled with some fairness as 'scenes of Pride or Pompousness'. But there is a value in the generalizing metaphor of Pride and Prejudice, as can be seen from the role of moral abstractions in Pope's *Moral Essays*. The *felt* ideas of Pride and Prejudice have a value in fixing the irony of many scenes in the novel. But this is not a matter of crude and overt reference as with the symbols of Ibsen.

It is not the title (except as any title sets up a rough expectation) that prepares us to view Mr Darcy's 'proud' acts as susceptible of another interpretation; it is rather the drama of the opening ballroom scene, with its harsh exhibit of the way 'character is decided' in this society:

> ...Mr Darcy soon drew the attention of the room by his fine, tall person, handsome features, noble mien; and the report which was in general circulation within five minutes after his entrance, of his having ten thousand a year. The gentlemen pronounced him to be a fine figure of a man, the ladies declared he was much handsomer than Mr Bingley, and he was looked at with great admiration for about half the evening, till his manners gave a disgust which turned the tide of his popularity; for he was discovered to be proud, to be above his company, and above being pleased; and not all his large estate in Derbyshire could then save him from having a most forbidding, disagreeable countenance, and being unworthy to be compared with his friend.
>
> ...His character was decided. He was the proudest, most disagreeable man in the world, and everybody hoped that he would never come there again.

Within the scenes which follow there is much neater and more particular definition of choices through brief but explicit comment. So in the scene at Sir William Lucas's house there is the observation of Mr Darcy's 'grave propriety' (his proud civility) over against the remark on his being 'not unwilling to receive' Elizabeth's hand. In the later dancing scene, the two views of Darcy's action are fixed as 'premeditated contempt' versus 'gallantry'. Though such defining labels are sparingly used and unobtrusively introduced, they are unmistakably there.

The choice of interpretations is sometimes defined only within a much larger context, but what is remarkable about Jane Austen is that the limitation can be so exactly located and settled. A rather bald example is the explanation given for the last of Mr Darcy's puzzling silences. On earlier occasions there has always been the unpleasant possibility that Darcy's silence was another sign of his want of genuine politeness. ('...his civility was so far awakened as to enquire of Elizabeth after the health of her family.') Now, even after the pleasant meetings at Pemberley, he seems to be rudely silent. He shows 'more thoughtfulness, and less anxiety to please'. Later in a direct statement to Elizabeth, Darcy gives a more favourable account of his odd behaviour:

'Why, especially [Elizabeth asks], when you called, did you look as if you did not care for me?'

'Because you were grave and silent, and gave me no encouragement.'

'But I was embarrassed.'

'And so was I.'

The alternative and pleasanter interpretation of Mr Darcy's character is sometimes brought out more obliquely by means of a later scene which merely supplies a new setting for a previous remark or action. Mr Darcy's remarks on his library seem in the context of the opening scenes sublimely smug, the simplest confirmation of our original prejudice:

'I am astonished,' said Miss Bingley, 'that my father should have left so small a collection of books. What a delightful library you have at Pemberley, Mr Darcy!'

'It ought to be good,' he replied, 'it has been the work of many generations.'

'And then you have added so much to it yourself, you are always buying books.'

'I cannot comprehend the neglect of a family library in such days as these.'

But Mr Darcy's words may be taken as coming from a proprietor, a man who has a just estimate of good things and a sense of his obligation as an inheritor of them. These possibilities, which seem remote enough when we first meet the above dialogue, become more than fancies as we read the scene in which Elizabeth is shown over Pemberley. Pemberley *was* a very 'good thing', reflecting the taste of the master who in his maintenance of the place and in his relations with his sister, his servants, and the villagers fulfilled all the responsibilities of a great proprietor.

It is important to note as another sign of the astute management of the novel, that in the original dialogue about libraries, as in many other instances, there is no direct comment which makes us take Darcy's behaviour in only an unpleasant sense. And when there is comment, as we have seen, it is mainly used to bring out the latent ambiguity without in any way resolving it. So, in general, the earlier Darcy scenes are left open in preparation for the climax of the book. At that point, Darcy does not have to be re-made, but 're-read'. The complete and rapid re-making of a character appears in an obvious form only in the later and lesser scenes of the novel.

The final definition of the possible views of Darcy's behaviour comes in the remarkable passage following Elizabeth's receipt of the letter from Darcy and in the similar passages on her thoughts after visiting Pemberley. The art of the book—which is another name for the control we have been describing—lies mainly in the preparation for these scenes and in the resolution within them of conflicting interpretations and attitudes. The passages connected with Darcy's letter present an odd, rather legalistic process. After the more obvious views of his behaviour and the possible alternatives are directly stated, the evidence on both sides is weighed and a reasonable conclusion is reached:

> After wandering along the lane for two hours, giving way to every variety of thought; re-considering events, determining probabilities, and reconciling herself as well as she could, to a change so sudden and so important, fatigue, and a recollection of her long absence, made her at length return home; . . .

To illustrate her manner of 'determining probabilities' we might take one of several examples of Darcy's pride. Immediately after Darcy has proposed to her, she describes his treatment of Jane in rather brutal language:

> . . . his pride, his abominable pride, his shameless avowal of what he had done with respect to Jane, his unpardonable assurance in acknowledging, though he could not justify it.

A little later, she reads Darcy's letter in which he explains that Jane had shown no 'symptom of peculiar regard' for Darcy. A 'second perusal' reminds Elizabeth that Charlotte Lucas had a similar opinion, and she acknowledges the justice of this account of Jane's outward behaviour. In much the same way she reviews other charges such as Darcy's injustice to Wickham or his objection to her own family's 'want of importance', and she is forced by the new evidence to draw 'more probable' conclusions.

Jane Austen does not make us suppose that Elizabeth has now simply discovered the 'real' Darcy or that an intricate person is easily known or known in his entirety, as is very clearly shown by Elizabeth's reply to Wickham's ironic questions about Darcy:

> . . . 'I dare not hope,' he continued in a lower and more serious tone, 'that he is improved in essentials.'
>
> 'Oh, no!' said Elizabeth. 'In essentials, I believe, he is very much what he ever was.'
>
> While she spoke, Wickham looked as if scarcely knowing whether to rejoice over her words, or to distrust their meaning. There was a something in her countenance which made him listen with an apprehensive and anxious attention, while she added,
>
> 'When I said that he improved on acquaintance, I did not mean that either his mind or manners were in a state of improvement, but that from knowing him better, his disposition was better understood.'

It is wise not to be dogmatic about 'essentials', since in any case they remain 'as they were'. A sensible person contents himself with 'better understanding', that is, with 'more reasonable' interpretations.

The judicial process by which Elizabeth 'determines probabilities' in reviewing Darcy's past actions is matched by the orderly way in which she later 'determines her feelings' toward him. [See *Pride and Prejudice,* towards the end of Chapter XLIV; 'As for Elizabeth . . . renewal of his addresses.' Please find the passage and read it through.]

In this beautifully graded progress of feeling, from 'hatred' or any 'dislike' to 'respect' to 'esteem' to 'gratitude' and a 'real interest' in Darcy's 'welfare', each sentiment is defined with an exactness which would be pedantic if separable from the habit of mind of Elizabeth (and of Jane Austen and the public she addressed).

If we refer these sentiments to the larger context of the novel, we shall see that each has also a dramatic definition which makes more precise the meaning given here. 'Respect', for example, points back to Elizabeth's reaction on discovering that Darcy had been just and honest in his relations with Jane and with Wickham. She had assured herself of his 'respectable' qualities through revising her judgment after reading his letter. 'Esteem'—'somewhat of a friendlier nature'— came when she visited Pemberley and learned of his qualities as land-lord and master: 'In what an amiable light does this place him!' thought Elizabeth. She had felt 'gratitude' after reading his letter, but only in the limited sense of being pleased at so flattering a proposal. 'Gratitude' in the wider sense it has here affected her first as she viewed Darcy's portrait: his 'regard' seemed to be turned particularly on her. She now finds especially 'gratifying' his behaviour to her aunt and uncle and his desire to introduce her to his sister. 'Gratitude' shades finally into an 'impression' which 'could not be exactly defined', a phrase which does not indicate a failure to make distinctions, but the recognition that finer distinctions are to be made. Elizabeth's response to Darcy is not just conventional 'love', but this special kind of gratitude. Her sister Jane is conventionally in love with a conven-tional lover. The dramatic equivalent of this distinction is Elizabeth's most lovable remark, 'she only smiles, I laugh'. Such a beautiful correspondence between explicit distinction and dramatic expression suddenly shows us what is meant by integrity of imagination.

Nothing in the novel, I think, makes more clear the degree and pervasiveness of the writer's control than the complete and precise definition of 'sentiments' which we have been describing. 'Artistic conscience', which like 'integrity of imagination' has become an almost meaningless term, finds again a meaning when referred to writing of this sort. Readers of eighteenth-century literature will want to add that such a fine sense of responsibility in the use of language, especially in the making of moral distinctions, does not belong to Jane Austen alone, but also to her family, to the eighteenth-century writers who were her teachers, and to her readers, who were prepared for such refinement 'even in a novel'.

The control without the sense of intricacy in character and without the resultant ironies would not be very remarkable. (The characters in a mediaeval interlude or an average thriller are 'beautifully defined' because there is so little sense of complexity.) So we may describe the relative inferiority of the latter third of *Pride and Prejudice* as a lowering in the awareness which makes the earlier parts of the novel so remarkable. There is no longer the same intricacy of character nor the same sense of the difficulty of finally 'knowing' a person. The change comes, as we should expect, in the part of the book which is most influenced by the conventions of melodramatic fiction: the country girl seduced by the rake, the search for the runaway lovers, the hero (wealthy and modest) who settles all financial problems, the proud parent (an aunt in this case) who makes a final attempt to part the hero and heroine, and a happy reunion with marriage.

In these later scenes Darcy and Elizabeth appear as less complex characters, and the explanation of their behaviour is made in simpler terms than in the measured reinterpretation at the climax of the book. . . .

'The Controlling Hand: Jane Austen and *Pride and Prejudice*', *Scrutiny*, Vol. XIII, September 1946, pp. 99–108 (99–111).

Persuasion: The Liberation of Feeling

... Anne is much more than Elinor and Fanny. These three do, indeed, share one distinction which no other major Austen character may claim: they are all unsubjected to the temper of Jane Austen's irony. In *Mansfield Park*, however, as in all her work previous to *Persuasion*, nothing has tempered her protagonists finely and vitally *except* irony; among her 'serious' heroines, Elinor is shadowy and blurred, Fanny a model of inappropriate priggish insipidity which cries out for the ironist. Only Anne survives without the dimension of irony. The third dimension of Jane Austen's heroines (except for the embarrassingly live, and finally snuffed out, Marianne) has been the author's irony or nothing at all; but Anne's depth—and her unique quality in the Austen gallery—is the sustained depth of projected and implicit personal emotion.

This emotion is not simply Anne aware of herself: she is discriminatingly aware of feeling, and capable of analyzing it with delicate accuracy; but it is as often the feeling of others (not just their principles or prospects, which the other heroines find far more engrossing) and the emotional atmosphere of groups and of places.

Unlike Emma or Elizabeth Bennet, she never imposes her tone upon others; nor in her shyness does she resemble Fanny, crouched fearfully in a corner and ready always with small, sharp teeth against a breach of propriety; for Anne seems to have withdrawn mainly by choice, and without prejudice to her awareness. Identity of interest is no longer prerequisite, as at Mansfield Park, to godliness: Anne has learned, between Kellynch and Uppercross, to accept the emotional disparateness of groups:

> Anne had not wanted this visit to Uppercross, to learn that a removal from one set of people to another, though at a distance of only three miles, will often include a total change of conversation, opinion, and idea. She had never been staying there before, without being struck by it, or without wishing that other Elliots could have her advantage in seeing how unknown, or unconsidered there, were the affairs which at Kellynch-hall were treated as of such general publicity and pervading interest; yet with all this experience, she believed she must now submit to feel that another lesson, in the art of knowing our own nothingness beyond our own circle, was become necessary for her.... (p. 42).

Deeply in love herself, she is capable of distinguishing without malice between love and what often passes for love; in the Musgrove sisters' attachment to Wentworth:

> ... while she considered Louisa to be rather the favourite, she could not but think, as far as she might dare to judge from memory and experience, that Captain Wentworth was not in love with either. They were more in love with him; yet there it was not love. It was a little fever of admiration; but it might, probably must, end in love with some (p. 82).

or in the sentimental Benwick's attachment to any girl available at the moment:

> He had an affectionate heart. He must love somebody (p. 167).

Anne is Jane Austen's first heroine to take a detailed and disinterested pleasure in sensory impressions; in the beauty of autumn:

> Her *pleasure* in the walk must arise from the exercise and the day, from the view of the last smiles of the year upon the tawny leaves and withered hedges, and from repeating to herself some few of the thousand poetical descriptions extant of autumn, that season of peculiar and inexhaustible influence on the mind of taste and tenderness, that season which has drawn from every poet, worthy of being read, some attempt at description, or some lines of feeling (p. 84).

in the 'romantic' attraction of Lyme (and it is remarkable that *Persuasion* is the first book in which Jane Austen uses the words 'romance' and 'romantic' without irony and in their favourable sense):

> ... the woody varieties of the cheerful village of Up Lyme, and, above all, Pinny, with its green chasms between romantic rocks, where the scattered forest trees and orchards of luxuriant growth declare that many a generation must have passed away since the first partial falling of the cliff prepared the ground for such a state ... (p. 95f).

These descriptions are perhaps the more revealing in their awkward and breathless, their almost travel-book style; for Jane Austen is opening compartments of her mind that have been shut till now, and she has not yet achieved the form most expressive of her new material. The fact remains that the world is enlarging—with some loss of hard, sharp contour initially, but with a great potential (and often realized) gain in variety and power.

Anne's devotion to Wentworth is, of course, the sustained emotional impulse of the book; and Anne traces it with unremitting sensitivity. Her feeling is clear enough in her first thought of him:

> ... Anne ... left the room, to seek the comfort of cool air for her

flushed cheeks; and as she walked along a favourite grove, said, with a gentle sigh, 'a few months more, and *he*, perhaps, may be walking here' (p. 25).

Without bitterness, but with a fixed regret, she recalls her decision, on Lady Russell's advice, to refuse him:

> ... Anne, at seven and twenty, thought very differently from what she had been made to think at nineteen (p. 29).
> How eloquent could Anne Elliot have been,—how eloquent, at least, were her wishes on the side of early warm attachment, and a cheerful confidence in futurity, against that over-anxious caution which seems to insult exertion and distrust Providence!—She had been forced into prudence in her youth, she learned romance as she grew older—the natural sequel of an unnatural beginning (p. 30).

If this last remark sounds to us irresistibly biographical, Jane Austen has only the tone of her earlier books, and the contrast of this late one, to blame.

Responding to an apparent reference to Wentworth,

> Anne hoped she had outlived the age of blushing; but the age of emotion she certainly had not (p. 49).

Continually she analyzes what she imagines his present feelings to be, and her hope rises or is depressed as she revolves what little evidence, favourable or unfavourable, she can gather:

> ... He must be either indifferent or unwilling. Had he wished ever to see her again, he need not have waited till this time ... (p. 58).
> He could not forgive her,—but he could not be unfeeling (p. 91).
> And, having ascended by imperceptible gradations of hope, she can at last allow herself to feel that he loves her still (p. 186).

Entering the room in which she meets Wentworth again for the first time in eight years, she must pass the first, and most unnerving, test:

> Her eye half met Captain Wentworth's; a bow, a curtsey passed; she heard his voice—he talked to Mary, said all that was right; said something to the Miss Musgroves, enough to mark an easy footing: the room seemed full—full of persons and voices—but a few minutes ended it (p. 59).

Events of the smallest scale take on breadth and depth. In a scene full of perilously balanced tensions and embarrassments, with Wentworth still uncomfortable in Anne's presence, and Charles Hayter sitting petulantly silent and hostile towards his supposed rival for Henrietta's hand, Anne kneels in attendance by a sick Musgrove child. His mischievous little brother persists in climbing upon her back, until suddenly she feels the child carried off and knows that Wentworth has done it:

> Her sensations on the discovery made her perfectly speechless. She could not even thank him. She could only hang over little Charles, with most disordered feelings. His kindness in stepping forward to her relief—the manner—the silence in which it had passed—the little particulars of the circumstance—with the conviction soon forced on her by the noise he was studiously making with the child, that he meant to avoid hearing her thanks, and rather sought to testify that her conversation was the last of his wants, produced such a confusion of varying, but very painful agitation, as she could not recover from, till enabled by the entrance of Mary and the Miss Musgroves to make over her little patient to their cares, and leave the room (p. 80).

And the effect is neither trivial nor sentimental, but ample and moving, because we have been convinced that it is not Anne's feeling which is limited but the life in which she has been imprisoned since Wentworth left. If she feels so minutely, it is because nothing remains to give her hope of happiness except the memory of Wentworth and such pathetic shreds of a relationship as he may now allow her. Anne comes near losing her hope, but she never loses the strength and dignity of her feeling.

When at last Jane Austen attends Anne on her walk to Mrs Smith's the morning after the concert, at which Wentworth betrayed his jealousy of Mr Elliot, we share the author's overt sympathy:

> Prettier musings of high-wrought love and eternal constancy, could never have passed along the streets of Bath, that Anne was sporting with from Camden-place to Westgate-buildings. It was almost enough to spread purification and perfume all the way (p. 192).

This burst of affection is relevant because Anne has already been created to such an ideal; the specific image here is incident, it expresses and illustrates—in a kind of objective valuation of her new joy—the Anne we already know.

It was not till her partial revision of *Persuasion* that Jane Austen permitted Anne to speak of feeling; but when Anne finally does speak, her sudden articulateness is the symbol of the new wide world which her confidence in Wentworth's reawakened love has thrown open to her, even as she looks back on the past and argues passionately with Captain Harville for the superior constancy of women:

> '... I should deserve utter contempt if I dared to suppose that true attachment and constancy were known only by woman. No, I believe you capable of everything great and good in your married

lives. I believe you equal to every important exertion, and to every domestic forbearance, so long as—if I may be allowed the expression, so long as you have an object. I mean, while the woman you love lives, and lives for you. All the privilege I claim for my own sex (it is not a very enviable one, you need not covet it) is that of loving longest, when existence or when hope is gone' (p. 235).

If the author is still too diffident to let Anne speak aloud her confession of love to Wentworth, their reunion is nevertheless a new thing for Jane Austen:

> There they exchanged again those feelings and those promises which had once before seemed to secure every thing, but which had been followed by so many, many years of division and estrangement. Then they returned again into the past, more exquisitely happy, perhaps, in their reunion, than when it had been first projected; more tender, more tried, more fixed in a knowledge of each other's character, truth, and attachment; more equal to act, more justified in acting. And there, as they slowly paced the gradual ascent, heedless of every group around them, seeing neither sauntering politicians, bustling housekeepers, flirting girls, nor nursery-maids and children, they could indulge in their retrospections and acknowledgments, and especially in those explanations of what had directly preceded the present moment, which were so poignant and so ceaseless in interest. All the little variations of the last week were gone through; and of yesterday and today there could scarcely be an end (p. 240f).

Elizabeth Bennet made a joke about having fallen in love with Pemberley. Emma's love the author summed up in the imperturbable catechism: 'What did she say? Just what a lady ought.' Fanny and Edmund faded mercifully out of sight before they pledged themselves to each other. And whether we agree that Anne's emotion 'proves not merely the biographical fact that Jane Austen had loved, but the aesthetic fact that she was no longer afraid to say so' (Virginia Woolf; see p. 27 of this present volume), we do know that Anne has experienced something which none of Jane Austen's previous heroines, by temperament or incident, even came near.

Persuasion is the story of Anne Elliot: its newness is in her sensitivity; its source and impulse are in her love of Wentworth; its limitations derive chiefly from her inconsistent limitations of vision, as if the author, dealing with a wholly different sort of heroine, was not yet able to exploit or even to recognize all the fresh possibilities arising. Consistent or inconsistent, however, Anne is perpetually at the centre of the novel. . . .

The central opposition in the novel is not, as both Mark Schorer and Miss Lascelles suggest, between false and true, or hidden and overt (though these are always in Jane Austen's background, and come to the fore in *Pride and Prejudice* and *Emma*); the problem of Anne and Wentworth is only a reflection, in personal terms, of a much more polarized opposition in the novel: a conflict between worlds.

Mansfield Park was the only other novel in which Jane Austen set up separate and irreconcilable worlds in conflict: but there the conception, though on her broadest and most imposing scale till then, was executed with a starched moral caution that introduced her hero and heroine stillborn and smothered her villains ruthlessly when their liveness was about to redirect the story. Jane Austen, in her regular pendulum swing to compunction, had determined to write a serious, a 'moral' book, and she recognized that the small, ironically conceived, personal tensions which had kept her earlier novels moving were not suitable to a serious subject; yet irony was still her only organizing impulse. Without irony, she could not organize her story around the figure of her heroine, she could not even make her heroine sympathetic; she could only set up her worlds and dispose of their inhabitants by means of an imported and arbitrary social judgment named Fanny Price. *Mansfield Park* failed as a work of art because its only sustaining impulse was external.

In *Persuasion,* not only is the conflict grander and more dramatic in conception; it is organized and resolved, gravely and unironically, in the feelings of the heroine. The conflict is between the feudal remnant, conscious of its tradition, and the rising middle class, conscious of its vitality, at the turn of the nineteenth century: between Sir Walter and Mr Elliot, between Lady Russell and Wentworth, between Mary Musgrove and her husband; and always at the centre, mediating directly or as an involved onlooker, is Anne Elliot.

In its mildest form, the conflict is observed reluctantly by Anne between Charles and Mary Musgrove. Mary has little energy to spare from her hypochondria, but what she has she devotes to upholding her notions of consequence, small scattered echoes of Sir Walter's grandiose self-congratulation. When her sister-in-law Henrietta seems preferred by Wentworth, Mary exclaims:

'... Dear me! If he should rise to any very great honours! If he should ever be made a Baronet! "Lady Wentworth" sounds very well. That would be a noble thing, indeed, for Henrietta! She would take place of me then, and Henrietta would not dislike that. Sir Frederick and Lady Wentworth! It would be but a new creation, however, and I never think much of your new creations' (p. 75).

She will not consider Charles Hayter as a possible suitor for Henrietta because 'she looked down very decidedly upon the Hayters' (p. 75). But her husband, who has no patience with mere mooning over rank, retorts with the hypnotic bourgeois incantation of advancement and property:

'Now you are talking nonsense, Mary. . . . It would not be a *great* match for Henrietta, but Charles has a very fair chance, through the Spicers, of getting something from the Bishop in the course of a year or two; and you will please to remember, that he is the eldest son; whenever my uncle dies, he steps into very pretty property. . . .' (p. 76).

Neither ever convinces the other, and neither ever feels the need to convince: Mary has her ailments to turn to; Charles is too contemptuous of his wife's logic, and too shallow and easy, to require more than an occasional 'Now you are talking nonsense, Mary.' The contrast is nevertheless basic and symbolic, for Charles can always offer well documented arguments in response to Mary's feeble snobbery: the ascendant middle class, whether freeholding farmer or (like Wentworth) free-booting sailor or adventurer or lawyer, knows where its strength lies, and is already talking down the enemy. This is their contrast; but their agreement signifies still more. Except for Charles's casual remark, buried in his statistics, that Charles Hayter is a 'good sort of fellow' (p. 76), neither Charles nor Mary makes a single reference to the personal qualities of the prospective suitors. Personality is never an issue.

Sir Walter is, of course, the epitome of blind blood-worship: feudalism in its last, inverted stage. Mr Elliot, nominally his heir but too impatient to wait for the honour, turns out finally to have been an adventurer seeking wealthy bourgeois respectability by the quickest means, according to Mrs Smith's revelation:

'Mr Elliot . . . at that period of his life, had one object in view—to make his fortune, and by a rather quicker process than the law. He was determined to make it by marriage. . . .' (p. 200f).

Later, having made his fortune by marriage, and having soon after providentially lost his wife, Mr Elliot returns to the pursuit of respectability by rank. The real opposition is here: Sir Walter, wishing simply to keep what he has, feels no need—indeed, has no talent—for cunning or aggressiveness (in business affairs, even his lawyer, Mr Shepherd, can lead him without much trouble); while Mr Elliot, who wished to get what he did not have, had to be both cunning and aggressive. But they also, like Charles and Mary, agree in their indifference to personality. Neither Sir Walter nor Mr Elliot moves out of the circle of his own possessive ego: Sir Walter sees everyone else as a possible foil, Mr Elliot sees everyone as a possible tool. And just as neither Mary nor Charles wins Anne over, so neither Sir Walter nor Mr Elliot gains her sympathy or is allowed any notion of what she feels.

The antagonism which chiefly engages Anne is, of course, that between Lady Russell and Wentworth. Anne loves them both, but to the end they are suspicious of each other. In view of their attitudes, this mutual distrust is not strange. Lady Russell is as much a supporter of title and tradition as Sir Walter:

> She had a cultivated mind, and was, generally speaking, rational and consistent—but she had prejudices on the side of ancestry; she had a value for rank and consequence, which blinded her a little to the faults of those who possessed them (p. 11).

Not only is she incapable of recognizing Sir Walter's fatuity, but she can be taken in by Mr Elliot's manner as soon as he assumes an outward respect for his uncle (p. 146f). Finally, she maintains a strong dislike of Wentworth:

> Such confidence, powerful in its own warmth, and bewitching in the wit which often expressed it, must have been enough for Anne; but Lady Russell saw it very differently.—His sanguine temper, and fearlessness of mind, operated very differently on her. She saw in it but an aggravation of the evil. It only added a dangerous character to himself. He was brilliant, he was headstrong.—Lady Russell had little taste for wit; and of any thing approaching to imprudence a horror. She deprecated the connexion in every light (p. 27).

For Wentworth possesses all the qualities calculated to offend a widow whose only stability is rank and family; all the new bourgeois virtues—confidence, aggressiveness, daring, an eye for money and the main chance. Even as a sailor, loving battle and glory, he is still frankly a businessman:

> 'Ah! those were pleasant days when I had the Laconia! How fast I made money in her.—A friend of mine, and I, had such a lovely cruise together off the Western Islands.—Poor Harville...! You know how much he wanted money—worse than myself. He had a wife....' (p. 67).

Battle and glory have their place and their excitement; but Wentworth and his fellow officers (and Jane Austen's sailor brothers) are far more excited at the prospect of a prize-ship or a promotion. Even kind Admiral Croft can scarcely think past a man's chances:

> 'I thought Captain Benwick a very pleasing young man,' said Anne....
> 'Oh! yes, yes, there is not a word to be said against James Benwick. He is only a commander, it is true, made last summer, and these are bad times for getting on, but he has not another fault that I know of...' (p. 171).

The irony is Jane Austen's; but the economic compulsion, the anxiety, is not only Admiral Croft's (habitually, by now) but Wentworth's. The Admiral loves his wife, Wentworth loves Anne; their problem has been to neutralize this anxiety—their own and that of the women they marry—without damage to their love. They are men of business, but they are men of feeling too; and their feeling survives its burden of middle-class anxiety and middle-class metaphor, just as Lady Russell's affection for Anne survives her immovable feudal prejudice.

Anne, then, can take no side in the conflict. For her, the only issue is feeling, whose survival—possible, though unlikely, on either side—is without bearing on the conflict itself. Lady Russell, Wentworth, and Admiral Croft—these are the persons to whom Anne warmly responds, and they are all persons whose feelings survive the economic battleground: even Lady Russell 'was a very good woman, and if her second object was to be sensible and well-judging, her first was to see Anne happy' (p. 249). Only Anne observes, from its centre, the whole history of the conflict that divides into two camps all the major characters of the book except herself; and her decision—which she made before the story begins—is that both sides are wrong. If it were not for Wentworth's return, however, she would have lived with her feelings unspoken and unfulfilled. Throughout the book, she is caught in the centre of a struggle whose issues—precedence, power, money, property—are hateful to her as issues, among people who pursue material goals in a wreckage of personality; and she will remain caught, forever, because she is a woman and unmarried in a society which maintains unmarried women on sufferance, because she has nowhere to go and nothing to say—unless the lover, not suitor but lover, whom she rejected in ignorance of his momentous distinction from the others, comes back to claim her. The worlds of Anne Elliot are not nearly so simple and definable as Fanny Price's, for Fanny could choose Mansfield Park and be sure of heaven. Anne has either no choice at all, or no need of choice: except in extremity, Sir Walter's world is hardly preferable to Mr Elliot's; and Wentworth, as she loves him and responds to his love, is outside the conflict altogether. Anne has learned that the conflict of her time engages objects and symbols, and that she can deal only with persons.

It is not that Anne escapes finally, but that she grows through and out of her prison. Understanding is prerequisite to growth and release, and understanding comes only within and through the pull of opposed tensions, even if these are pulling away from personality: the conflict must be gone through before it can be evaluated and rejected. Having gone through it in eight years of accumulating observation and judgment, Anne has grown to understand just how rare a lover Wentworth is; but she has learned, even more sombrely, how rare love is, and if she has decided, after her ordeal, that our first duty is—more than to ourselves or to immediate inclination—to *all* who love us, we may accept, in her joyous present, her charitably strict application of this truth to Lady Russell's mistake:

'...I must believe that I was right, much as I suffered from it, that I was perfectly right in being guided by the friend whom you will love better than you do now. To me she was in the place of a parent.... I am not saying that she did not err in her advice.... But I mean, that I was right in submitting to her, and that if I had done otherwise, I should have suffered more in continuing the engagement than I did even in giving it up, because I should have suffered in my conscience' (p. 246)....

There are ... comic scenes and comic characters in *Persuasion;* but its inner orbit and final effect are not comic. 'The comic poet,' says George Meredith, 'is in the narrow field, or enclosed square, of the society he depicts; and he addresses the still narrower enclosure of men's intellects, with reference to the operation of the social world upon their characters.' (*An Essay on Comedy and The Uses of The Comic Spirit,* N.Y., 1897, pp. 79f). This might well have been written with Jane Austen's comedies in mind; but it is precisely here that *Persuasion* diverges, for *Persuasion* is concerned, not focally with the operation of the social world upon men's characters, but with the emotional resistance that men put up against the perpetual encroachments of the social world. The whole pattern of the novel is one, not of delusion and face-saving (as in *Emma* or *The Egoist*), but of resistance and tension. Statically, *Persuasion* offers a figure caught between pairs of opposites: Anne between Sir Walter and Mr Elliot, between Mary and Charles, between Lady Russell and Wentworth. The course of the story shows how she was caught and how she is finally able to transcend the conflict. The interest of the story is to illustrate the plight of a sensitive woman in a society which has a measure for everything except sensitivity. And the climax of the story occurs when Anne—Jane Austen's only heroine so aware of, and so irrevocably cut off from, her society—is ready to articulate and define her lonely personal triumph.

So Wentworth is enlightened, and Anne is freed, as the novel rounds to its authentic climax at the White Hart Inn, where Anne can speak at last what she is now so sure of, after eight years. The perfection and emotional resonance of this scene are unique in Jane Austen's work: nowhere else do we grasp so much of personality grown and summed up. Unlike Elizabeth Bennet and Emma, who did not grow except in our aggregating perception of them, bit by bit, through the perspective of the author's irony; unlike Fanny Price and Elinor, who had not even this ironically simulated growth—Anne has grown altogether and truly, out of the constrictions of her group, out of her timidity, out of the defiant need for wit and self-assertion, out of the author's tight, ironic feminine world. *Persuasion* has a new impulse, feeling; and a new climax, self-fulfilment....

Jane Austen: Irony as Defense and Discovery, Princeton University Press, Princeton N.J., 1952, pp. 222–8, 231–7, 239–40.

Two Solitary Heroines

... All four heroines [Catherine, Marianne, Elizabeth and Emma] painfully, though with varying degrees of pain, discover that they have been making mistakes both about themselves and about the world in which they live. All their *data* have to be reinterpreted. Indeed, considering the differences of their situations and characters, the similarity of the process in all four is strongly marked. All realize that the cause of the deception lay within; Catherine, that she had brought to the Abbey a mind 'craving to be frightened', Marianne, that 'her own feelings had prepared her sufferings', Elizabeth, that she has 'courted ignorance' and 'driven reason away', Emma, that she has been practising deceptions on herself. Self-hatred or self-contempt, though (once more) in different degrees, are common to all. Catherine 'hated herself'; Marianne abhors herself; Elizabeth finds her conduct 'despicable'; Emma gives hers 'every bad name in the world'. Tardy and surprising self-knowledge is presented in all four, and mentioned by name in the last two. 'I never knew myself,' says Elizabeth; Emma's conduct and 'her own heart' appear to her, unwelcome strangers both, 'in the same few minutes'. . . .

In *Mansfield Park* and *Persuasion* the heroine falls into no such self-deception and passes through no such awakening. We are, it is true, given to understand that Anne Elliot regards the breaking off of her early engagement to Wentworth as a mistake. If any young person now applied to her for advice in such circumstances, 'they would never receive any of such certain immediate wretchedness and uncertain future good'. For Anne in her maturity did not hold the view which Lord David Cecil attributes to Jane Austen, that 'it was wrong to marry for money, but it was silly to marry without it'. She was now fully 'on the side of early warm attachment, and a cheerful confidence in futurity, against that over-anxious caution which seems to insult exertion and distrust Providence'. (Notice, in passing, the Johnsonian cadence of a sentence which expresses a view that Johnson in one of his countless moods might have supported.) But though Anne thinks a mistake has been made, she does not think it was she that made it. She declares that she was perfectly right in being guided by Lady Russell who was to her 'in the place of a parent'. It was Lady Russell who had erred. There is no true parallel here between Anne and the heroines we have been considering. Anne, like Fanny Price, commits no errors.

Having placed these two novels apart from the rest because they do not use the pattern of 'undeception', we can hardly fail to notice that they share another common distinction. They are the novels of the solitary heroines.

Catherine Morland is hardly ever alone except on her journey from Northanger Abbey, and she is soon back among her affectionate, if placid, family. Marianne Dashwood bears her own painful secret without a confidant for a time; but her isolation, besides being temporary, is incomplete; she is surrounded by affection and respect. Elizabeth always has Jane, the Gardiners, or (to some extent) her father. Emma is positively spoiled; the acknowledged centre of her own social world. Of all these heroines we may say, as Jane Austen says of some other young women, 'they were of consequence at home and favourites abroad'.

But Fanny Price and Anne are of no 'consequence'. The consciousness of 'mattering' which is so necessary even to the humblest women, is denied them. Anne has no place in the family councils at Kellynch Hall; 'she was only Anne'. She is exploited by her married sister, but not valued; just as Fanny is exploited, but not valued, by Mrs Norris. Neither has a confidant; or if Edmund had once been a confidant as well as a hero to Fanny, he progressively ceases to be so. Some confidence, flawed by one vast forbidden topic, we may presume between Anne and Lady Russell; but this is almost entirely off stage and within the novel we rarely see them together. Both heroines come within easy reach of one of the great archetypes— Cinderella, Electra. Fanny, no doubt, more so. She is almost a Jane Austen heroine condemned to a Charlotte Brontë situation. We do not even believe in what Jane Austen tells us of her good looks; whenever we are looking at the action through Fanny's eyes, we feel ourselves sharing the consciousness of a plain woman.

Even physically, we see them alone; Fanny perpetually in the East Room with its fireless grate and its touching, ridiculous array of petty treasures (what Cinderella, what Electra, is without them?) or Anne, alone beside the hedge, an unwilling eavesdropper, Anne alone with her sick nephew, Anne alone in the empty house waiting for the sound of Lady Russell's carriage. And in their solitude both heroines suffer; far more deeply than Catherine, Elizabeth, and Emma, far more innocently than Marianne. Even Elinor suffers less. These two novels, we might almost say, stand to the others as Shakespeare's 'Dark' comedies to his comedies in general. The difference in the lot of the heroines goes with a difference in the 'character parts'. Mrs Norris is almost alone among Jane Austen's vulgar old women in being genuinely evil, nor are her greed and cruelty painted with the high spirits which make us not so much hate as rejoice in Lady Catherine de Bourgh.

These solitary heroines who make no mistakes have, I believe—or had while she was writing—the author's complete approbation. This is connected with the unusual pattern of *Mansfield Park* and *Persuasion*. The heroines stand almost outside, certainly a little apart from, the world which the action of the novel depicts. It is in it, not in them, that self-deception occurs. They see it, but its victims do not. They do not of course stand voluntarily apart, nor do they willingly accept the role of observers and critics. They are shut out and are compelled to observe: for what they observe, they disapprove.

It is this disapproval which, though shared both by Fanny and Anne, has perhaps drawn on Fanny, from some readers, the charge of being a prig. I am far from suggesting that Fanny is a successful heroine, still less that she is the equal of Anne. But I hardly know the definition of *Prig* which would make her one. If it means a self-righteous person, a Pharisee, she is clearly no prig. If it means a 'precisian', one who adopts or demands a moral standard more exacting than is current in this own time and place, then I can see no evidence that Fanny's standard differs at all from that by which Marianne condemns herself or Anne Elliot corrects Captain Benwick. Indeed, since Anne preaches while Fanny feels in silence, I am a little surprised that the charge is not levelled against Anne rather than Fanny. For Anne's *chastoiement* of poor Benwick is pretty robust; 'she ventured to recommend a larger allowance of prose in his daily study, and ... mentioned such works of our best moralists, such collections of the finest letters, such memoirs of characters of worth and suffering, as occurred to her at the moment as calculated to rouse and fortify the mind by the highest precepts and the strongest examples of moral and religious endurances' (Chap. xi). Notice, too, the standards which Anne was using when she first began to suspect her cousin, Mr Elliot: 'she saw that there had been bad habits; that Sunday travelling had been a common thing; that there had been a period of his life (and probably not a short one) when he had been at least careless on all serious matters.' Whatever we may think of these standards ourselves, I have not the least doubt that they are those of all the heroines, when they are most rational, and of Jane Austen herself. This is the hard core of her mind, the Johnsonian element, the iron in the tonic.

How, then, does Fanny Price fail? I suggest, by insipidity. *Pauper videri Cinna vult et est pauper.* One of the most dangerous of literary ventures is the little, shy, unimportant heroine whom none of the other characters value. The danger is that your readers may agree with the other characters. Something must be put into the heroine to make us feel that the other characters are wrong, that she contains depths they never dreamed of. That is why Charlotte Brontë would have succeeded better with Fanny Price. To be sure, she would have ruined everything else in the book; Sir Thomas and Lady Bertram and Mrs Norris would have been distorted from credible types of pompous dullness, lazy vapidity and vulgar egoism into fiends complete with horns, tails and rhetoric. But through Fanny there would have blown a storm of passion which made sure that we at least would never think her insignificant. In Anne, Jane Austen did succeed. Her passion (for it is not less), her insight, her maturity, her prolonged fortitude, all attract us. But into Fanny, Jane Austen, to counterbalance her apparent insignificance, has put really nothing except rectitude of mind; neither passion, nor physical courage, nor wit, nor resource. Her very love is only calf love—a schoolgirl's hero-worship for a man who has been kind to her when they were both children, and who, incidentally, is the least attractive of all Jane Austen's heroes. Anne gains immensely by having for her lover almost the best. In real life, no doubt, we continue to respect interesting women despite the preposterous men they sometimes marry. But in fiction it is usually fatal. Who can forgive Dorothea for marrying such a sugarstick as Ladislaw, or Nellie Harding for becoming Mrs Bold? Or, of course, David Copperfield for his first marriage?

Fanny also suffers from the general faults of *Mansfield Park*, which I take to be, if in places almost the best, yet as a whole the least satisfactory, of Jane Austen's works. I can accept Henry Crawford's elopement with Mrs Rushworth: I cannot accept his intention of marrying Fanny. Such men never make such marriages.

But though Fanny is insipid (yet not a prig) she is always 'right' in the sense that to her, and to her alone, the world of *Mansfield Park* always appears as, in Jane Austen's view, it really is. Undeceived, she is the spectator of deceptions. These are made very clear. In Chap. ii we learn that the Bertram girls were 'entirely deficient' in 'self-knowledge'. In Chap. iii Sir Thomas departs for Antigua without much anxiety about his family because, though not perfectly confident of his daughters' discretion, he had ample trust 'in Mrs Norris's watchful attention and in Edmund's judgment'. Both, of course, failed to justify it. In Chap. xii when Crawford was absent for a fortnight it proved 'a fortnight of such dullness to the Miss Bertram's as ought to have put them both on their guard'. Of course it did not. In Chap. xvi when Edmund at last consents to act, Fanny is forced to raise the question, 'was he not deceiving himself'. In Chap. xxxiv when Crawford (whose manners are insufferable) by sheer persistence pesters Fanny into speech when she has made her desire for silence obvious, she says, 'Perhaps, Sir, I thought it was a pity you did not always know yourself as you seemed to do at that moment.' But deception is most fully studied in the person of Mary Crawford, 'a mind led astray and bewildered, and without any suspicion of being so: darkened, yet fancying itself light'. The New Testament echo in the language underlines the gravity of the theme. It may be that Jane Austen has not treated it successfully. Some think that she hated Mary and falsely darkened a character whom she had in places depicted as charming. It might be the other way round; that the author, designing to show deception at its height, was anxious to play fair, to show how the victim could be likeable at times, and to render her final state the more impressive by raising in us false hopes that she might have been cured. Either way, the gap between Mary at her best and Mary in her last interview with Edmund is probably too wide; too wide for fiction, I mean, not for possibility. (We may have met greater inconsistency in real life; but real life does not need to be probable.) That last interview, taken by itself, is an alarming study of human blindness. We may—most of us do—disagree with the standards by which Edmund condemns Mary. The dateless and universal possibility in the scene is Mary's invincible ignorance of what those standards are. All through their conversation she is cutting her own throat. Every word she speaks outrages Edmund's feeling 'in total ignorance, unsuspiciousness of there being such feelings' (Chap. xlvii). At last, when we feel that her ghastly innocence (so to call it) could go no further, comes the master stroke. She tries to call him back by 'a saucy, playful smile'. She still thought that possible. The misunderstanding is incurable. She will never know Edmund.

In *Persuasion* the theme of deception is much less important. Sir Walter is, no doubt, deceived both in his nephew and in Mrs Clay, but that is little more than the mechanism of the plot. What we get more of is the pains of the heroine in her role of compelled observer. Something of this had appeared in Elinor Dashwood, and more in Fanny Price, constantly forced to witness the courtship of Edmund and Mary Crawford. But Fanny had also, at times, derived amusement from her function of spectator. At the rehearsals of *Lovers' Vows* she was 'not unamused to observe the selfishness which, more or less disguised, seemed to govern them all' (Chap. xiv). It is a kind of pleasure which we feel sure that Jane Austen herself had often enjoyed. But whether it were that something in her own life now began to show her less of the spectator's joys and more of his pains, forcing her on from 'as if we were God's spies' to 'break my heart for I must hold my tongue', or that she is simply exploring a new literary vein, it certainly seems that Anne's unshared knowledge of the significance of things she hears and sees is nearly always in some degree painful. At Kellynch she has 'a knowledge which she often wished less, of her father's character'. At the Musgroves 'One of the least agreeable circumstances of her residence ... was her being treated with too much confidence by all parties, and being too much in the secret of the complaints of each house' (Chap. vi). One passage perhaps gives the real answer to any charge of priggery that might lie against her or Fanny for the judgments they pass as spectators. Speaking of Henrietta's behaviour to Charles Hayter, Jane Austen says that Anne 'had delicacy which must be pained' by it (Chap. ix). This is not so much like the Pharisee's eagerness to condemn as the musician's involuntary shudder

at a false note. Nor is it easily avoided by those who have standards
of any sort. Do not our modern critics love to use the term 'embarrassing' of literature which violently offends the standards of their own
group? and does not this mean, pretty nearly, a 'delicacy' on their
part which 'must be pained'? But of course all these spectator's
pains sink into insignificance beside that very special, almost
unendurable, pain which Anne derives from her understanding of
Wentworth's every look and word. For *Persuasion*, from first to last,
is, in a sense in which the other novels are not, a love story....

'A Note on Jane Austen', *Essays in Criticism*, Vol. IV, October
1954, pp. 362–9 (359–71).

Jane Austen's *Emma*

'Jane Austen,' said Henry James in one of his few great misjudgments 'was instinctive and charming. . . . For signal examples of what composition, distribution, arrangement can do, of how they intensify the life of a work of art, we have to go elsewhere.' We do not, of course; and my purpose here is to suggest something of the complexity of the structure that Jane Austen creates to express the elaborate pattern of values contained in *Emma*. 'I am going to take a heroine whom no-one but myself will much like,' said Jane Austen of the novel; and one might set the remark against her comment that Anne Elliot, the heroine of *Persuasion* (surely Jane Austen's best novel) was almost too good for her. It is presumably a moral objection she fears will be brought against Emma; and it is to be by resolving this situation—by fitting Emma in to the moral expectations which she projects outwards into the audience, as it were—that the book must work. The self-willed quality of Emma, in which her attractiveness for reader and for novelist resides, must be contained and adapted, adapted to a norm which is neither social (though it is a norm which *lives* in society) nor doctrinaire (though it is a norm pragmatic simply in the sense that it re-establishes by proof of value the best traditional decencies).

Jane Austen is concerned with two kinds of world—the social world and the moral world—and their interaction, an interaction that is intimate, but also complex. It is often complained of her that she measured life from the conventional social standards of the upper middle class about which she writes and to which she belongs, and that this limits her wider relevance and 'excludes' her from the modern novel, one of the attributes of which is a greater range in its treatment of character and value. Leavis disposes of one aspect of this idea in *The Great Tradition*, and it is worth stressing here the degree to which she dissipates and tests her own predilections, and is capable of having predilections that seem to violate the rigidities we associate with her. Of course it is true that class attitudes are of the greatest importance; but it is in the evaluation of these attitudes, and the building up of a scale of them for the proper conduct of the moral life, that she excels. She is nothing if not stringent. The whole structure of her inventions is recurrently that of a kind of moral assault course, an extended interview in which candidates give their qualifications, undergo a succession of tests, and are finally rewarded by the one prize that is possible and appropriate in their social context—

marriage, a marriage which is aesthetically right, morally and humanly balanced, financially sound. (Lawrence in some of his novels uses a similar structure, the tests here being emotional and sexual, the final reward genital.)

What Jane Austen has to do, then, in *Emma* is to establish side by side a social world and a moral world, the latter setting up a higher level of action and judgment than the former. The social world is carefully and precisely given; it is elaborate in range, though not in class. The action takes place in Highbury, a 'large and prosperous village, almost amounting to a town', sixteen miles out of London; its life is the life of the time of writing (*Emma* was published in 1816). The landscape of Highbury is a landscape of property; there is Hartfield, the home of the Woodhouses, who are 'the first in consequence in Highbury'; there is Randalls, home of Mr Weston, 'a little estate'; there is Donwell Abbey 'in the parish adjoining, the seat of Mr Knightley'. Emma's sister lives in London, in Brunswick Square, only relatively accessible; Highbury is a more or less self-contained social unit, and it certainly contains most of the action. Further, the upper middle-class level of Highbury life includes most of the significant characters; and this is the level we see from. There are persons of higher rank, but they are *felt* to be high—in particular, the Churchills, the great Yorkshire family, are presented as rather 'above' the novel. There are, too, characters clearly 'below' the novel like the tenant-farmer Robert Martin and the former Miss Taylor and Mrs Goddard and Miss Bates, who come from the depressed 'professional' middle class. And then there are the socially indeterminate characters, who serve so importantly in the action—Miss Harriet Smith, illegitimate, of obscure origins, unfixed by kinship or duty; Frank Churchill, split between families; and Jane Fairfax. These figures, coming from outside the locale and existing in uncertain relation to it, are the disturbing forces; and their presence promotes most of the action. In particular Miss Harriet Smith is an anarchic force and, especially, a test of people's observations of innate quality, because she can fit in at any of a number of possible class levels; indeed, she can claim her class by her own merits, and so is in the singular position of being mobile in a largely stable society. And the novel, by concentrating on the period prior to marriage in these people, is able to show them at their most mobile; they exist in a state of uncertainty, finished by marriage, which 'fixes' them at a deserved level in the class system.

Now the central characters of the fiction are landowners with tenant farmers, persons of private income, or persons dependent on the professions or trade; they are small in number in the novel, and are concentrated in houses and families, with few points of reference outside Highbury; they live in a controlled and stable world. Most of the characters know one another before the action of the novel

begins and enlarge existing relationships in the course of it; they are
related by kinship or common social duties; they live most of their
lives in the place where they are born. The limits of the world of the
novel are, indeed, determined from the centre—all the characters
exist in some kind of established relationship to the heroine or her
immediate friends. In picaresque novels the relationships with the
hero are usually those of casual encounter, a structure that is con-
sonant with a pragmatic and open view of the universe; but here we
have a homogeneous world, taking its standards of life from within
itself, and communicating outside only rarely. The characters are
inhibited by a strong sense of rank and social duty, and no real
violation of rank is within the novel's probabilities. The Highbury
equals are capable of intimate relationships with one another; but, as
rank changes, the relation to the Woodhouses grows more distant
(the vicar is not close, the schoolmistress is received, the poor are
visited), while characters in mobile situations create most of the
tensions—like the rising Coles: 'The Coles were very respectable in
their way, but they ought to be taught that it was not for them to
arrange the terms on which superior families would visit them.' (But
this is by no means the *final* standard of judgment; the thought is
Emma's, and the reader is invited soon to wonder, when he meets the
Coles and finds their pleasantness stressed, what constitutes
'superiority'.) The constraints of a fixed society are firmly felt, and
Jane Austen never tests the values that arise within this world outside
the area in which they are possible (in industrial cities or in lower
social brackets); there is no need to; in this agrarian and hierarchical
world, subscribing by assent to a stylized system of properties and
duties, she finds a context in which they can yield their full resources.

The society in which the moral action takes place is then a local,
limited, stylized world, with its own operative values and its own
occasions. Its social intercourse is unelaborate. When people meet
they do so over dinner or at balls or in Ford's shop; encounters occur
by formal arrangement; there are few accidental meetings, and so
precise are the circumstances of this life that when these occur (as
when Harriet meets Robert Martin in the shop) they are deeply
disturbing. Persons stand out large, while the formalities make for a
controlled universe, in which our own sense of propriety as readers is
engaged to the degree that, when Jane Fairfax and Frank Churchill
are, by a conjunction of accidents, left alone with the sleeping Miss
Bates and this 'breach' goes unobserved, we alone are called on to
observe it and reflect on its significance. The degree of social stability,
the preciseness of social expectations, the limitations on eccentric
behaviour or concealments or violent action, reinforce and make
significant the moral order. They enable a concentration on the
quality of the individual life. They create a high degree of consensus
about behaviour—about what constitutes decent action. They provide

a relatively closed and rounded world in which, once a level of adequate living has been acquired, it can be reinforced from without, for the future will be reasonably like the present.

Within these limits, though, the society throws up a broad range of values, out of which the tensions of the novel arise. The characters think about similar things, but they think differently about them. They think differently about the importance of rank, about the relative value of taste or courtesy or honour, and about the importance of reason or emotion in conduct. Certain things are commonly approved or frowned upon—frivolity is disliked and goodwill valued—while on other matters different characters take different stands. And this is the way in which we are coerced by the novelist into perceiving and adopting a measure, for, either through direct authorial intervention or more commonly by the relative elevation and demotion of various characters, this latter done by a complex strategy and tone, we perceive a pattern. The public values are placed according to a private and, as I've said, an interestingly pragmatic view. People define themselves by their actions, and as they act we perceive that there are in the novel superior and inferior people in moral as well as social terms. The social order yields to the moral. The morally inferior people tend in fact to be socially high, to considerable dramatic effect; Emma herself, at the beginning, is one of them and Frank Churchill another, while people of lower rank, like the Martins and the Coles, elevate themselves by their actions. In this fashion certain values emerge as positive—particularly values having to do with care and respect for others, the decent discharge of one's duties, and the scrupulous improvement of oneself. They are values associated with, but by no means intrinsic to, an upper middle-class social position. So frivolity may be despised, but accomplishments count high, since they evidence self-discipline and self-enlargement and please others—the fact that Mr Martin reads is highly in his favour in this emergent scale, while Harriet Smith's taking a long time to choose materials at Ford's is not in hers. A friendly and social disposition is valued, but not *too* highly, since Emma's criticism of Jane Fairfax's reserve comes to tell more against Emma than it does against Jane and, what is more, it blinds her to some of the excellence of Mr Knightley. Goodwill and a contented temper are valued, but have their associated failures—Mr Weston is too easy-going for reasonable living, and Emma at once too indulgent over moral matters and not indulgent enough over social ones. To be 'open, straight-forward and well judging', like Martin, is important, but not as important as the rewarding side of Mr Knightley's more closed and critical temper. All this is the central area of the action, for it is what is at issue between Knightley and Emma; and yet we do come to value Emma's warmth and openness, only wanting it placed and ordered.

Birth and good manners are important, but only when there is something behind them. Elegance is admired, highly by Emma, less so by others. Mr Elton is 'self-important, presuming, familiar, ignorant and ill-bred'; the observations are Emma's, and have to be mediated by us carefully, for they show up Mr Elton and Emma. This picking up of tone is most important for the book, and we are helped by alternative views—for instance, Jane Fairfax is more tolerant of Mr Elton. Mr Weston is a little too open-hearted for Emma—'General benevolence, and not general friendship, make a man what he ought to be. She could fancy such a man.' To Harriet she commends 'the habit of self-command', but responds to Harriet's 'tenderness of heart' —'There is nothing to be compared to it. Warmth and tenderness of heart, with an affectionate, open manner, will beat all clearness of head in the world for attraction.' But Mr Knightley, in one of the debates in which the education of Emma—and to a lesser extent of Knightley himself—is conducted and in which a permissible range of *difference* of value is reconciled, offers a more rational and mature view; he states the case for a plan of life strictly adhered to, a sense of duty and of courtesy, and a right realization of what one owes to one's social situation and therefore one's function. This competition of values between Knightley and Emma, which is one of our main guides to the direction of the book, touches on other issues and other people, of course—an interesting example of its method being the way in which Knightley reappraises Emma's description of Churchill as 'amiable':

'... No, Emma; your amiable young man can be amiable only in French, not in English. He may be very "aimable", have very good manners, and be very agreeable; but he can have no English delicacy towards the feelings of other people—nothing really amiable about him.'

Other issues come into these debates, to add to the dense moral atmosphere. Thus Churchill is criticized early for being above his connections, later for being too exuberant; while he himself criticizes 'civil falsehoods', but employs them. Emma admires elegance highly; she has a practical, advantage-seeking view of attractive qualities in people; she criticizes Mr Knightley for inventing lines of conduct that are not practical. Mr Knightley reverses this case, condemns Emma's fancy and whim, and recommends 'judging by nature'. In consequence, the moral life is in the front of the characters' minds throughout; it is *linked* with class—as in the description of the estate at Donwell Abbey as belonging to 'a family of such true gentility, untainted in blood *and understanding*'—but understanding is insistently prior to blood as the notion of gentility begins to take a kind of ideal shape.

And so from the very first page of the book we are conscious of a disparity between the moral and the social scale. Emma's situation is, from the start, shown to be happy—

> Emma Woodhouse, handsome, clever, and rich, with a comfortable home and a happy disposition, seemed to unite some of the best blessings of existence, and had lived nearly twenty-one years in the world with little to distress or vex her.

But the complexities of the handling are already present. There is the hint, offered through nuances of diction, that the 'best blessings of existence' only *seem* to be hers; there is the point, further taken up and insisted on, that she has not been vexed but rather over-indulged. Her father is 'affectionate, indulgent'; her governess has 'a mildness of temper' that 'had hardly allowed her to impose any restraint', and presently by an explicit statement Jane Austen converts the hints into a direct moral observation—'The real evils, indeed, of Emma's situation were the power of having rather too much of her own way, and a disposition to think a little too well of herself.'

A distinction is to be made between social and moral 'success', then; and this is reinforced when we are told, for instance, of the history of Mr Weston's previous marriage into a family of high rank, which

> was an unsuitable connection, and did not produce much happiness. Mrs Weston ought to have found more in it, for she had a husband whose warm heart and sweet temper made him think everything due to her in return for the great goodness of being in love with him; but though she had one sort of spirit, she had not the best. She had resolution enough to pursue her own will in spite of her brother, but not enough to refrain from unreasonable regrets . . .

The moral scale is centred rather particularly, throughout, upon what is reasonable and desirable in a social life whose basic unit is the family, what makes for good and open dealing between people, prospers and opens their relationships and makes them dutiful and considerate in all their public actions. Jane Austen's novels are domestic novels, novels centred on marriage; most of the commentary and moral discussion is in fact directed toward defining the conditions for a good marriage, and preparing the one good marriage which contrasts with all others in the novel and so dominates it. But marriage is a social pact and so must answer to the public dimension. The general expectations of this book are that people will make the marriages they deserve, and that the climax will be Emma's marriage, made when she has answered to her faults and resolved her dilemmas.

Whom, then, will Emma marry? This is the question on which the plot turns. This plot, simply summarized, is concerned with a girl of many fine qualities but of certain considerable errors deriving from the misuse of her own powers, who realizes these errors, perceives that they have made her make false attributions of worth to the people in her circle and, repenting, marries the man who can instruct her in an accurate reaction to the world. The first part of the plot, the Aristotelian 'beginning', takes us to Chapter 17. In this section Emma is a detached agent in someone else's destiny; this is that part of the novel concerned with Emma's attempt to intervene in the life of Harriet Smith by marrying her to Mr Elton, and its function is to demonstrate the nature of Emma's mistakes about the world, and the dangers of detached and desultory action. By the time we reach Chapters 16 and 17, where we are presented with Emma's regrets, we have all we need in the way of moral direction for the rest of the book. Mr Knightley's interpretation of character and event has been shown to be better than Emma's, and we have a clear sense of Emma's tendency to misread what is before her, as well as of the faults, particularly snobbery and whimsy, which make her do this. The use of Harriet Smith as a device to expose the two different versions of the world espoused by Emma and Mr Knightley is singularly skilful. For Harriet's illegitimacy means that she can be judged very differently by different people; and each of them associate her with a rank that indicates the nature of their judgment. The uncertainty about Harriet's background thus becomes a dramatic delaying device, and much depends on the discovery of her true station, for then we shall see who is correct about her. The point is, as I have indicated, that her statement of herself, unlike that of any other characters in the book, depends entirely upon her *own* attributes; she is not reinforced by any class position. And so the question that arises is—is it Emma who is snobbish about Mr Martin, and damaging to Harriet in seeking to link her with Mr Elton; or is it Mr Knightley who is snobbish in his assumption that she deserves no better than Mr Martin, and that she is harmful company for Emma? The matter goes further—for to Emma Harriet has the virtues which commend a woman to men (beauty and good nature) and with these she has all she needs to win affection. But Mr Knightley sees the marriage connection as involving larger issues—

> 'Men of sense, whatever you may choose to say, do not want silly wives. Men of family would not be very fond of connecting themselves with a girl of such obscurity...'

The beautifully managed scene where Knightley puts this to Emma, and dissipates any feeling we may have of *his* snobbery by talking of Robert Martin's 'sense, sincerity and good humour' and his 'true gentility' of mind, is quickly supported by his being proved right about Mr Elton—

> 'Depend upon it. Elton will not do... Elton may talk sentimentally,

but he will act rationally. He is as well acquainted with his own claims as you can be with Harriet's.'

Indeed, Knightley's criticism of Emma's behaviour has a precise moral tenor; he points to a specific fault—'If you were as much guided by nature in your estimate of men and women, and as little under the power of fancy and whim in your dealings with them as you are where these children were concerned, we might always think alike.' That Emma *is* guided by fancy and whim we begin to see the more when, after a succession of delightfully handled comic scenes founded on the ambiguity of Mr Elton's supposed wooing of Harriet, Mr John Knightley points out to Emma that Mr Elton seems to have an interest in her. Emma's response is clearly self-deluding:

> ... She walked on, amusing herself in the consideration of the blunders which often arise from a partial knowledge of circumstances, of the mistakes which people of high pretensions to judgment are for ever falling into, and not very well pleased with her brother for imagining her blind and ignorant, and in want of counsel.

The irony is turned directly against her; and her ignorance on the matter, her failure to perceive that it is *she* who is being courted by Mr Elton, takes on a dimension beyond the comic—takes on the status of a moral fault.

The second part of the novel, the 'middle', is that concerned with Emma's mistakes about the nature of Frank Churchill's and Jane's characters, and her inability to infer the truth here because of her pre-judgments. The situations are now more complicated, but Emma repeats her errors without real improvement, inventing a romance before she has even met her between Jane and Mr Dixon, and another between Churchill and herself. Here the purpose of the action is to show how she behaves in events which increasingly come to involve not a protégée, but her own destiny, to show how she is capable of misusing herself. This part of the plot ends with a significant and crucial discovery, Emma's discovery that she is in love.

The 'end' of the book beautifully enforces the weight and meaning of the book; the waters clear, and all the significances are laid bare in a simple delaying action which enables Jane Austen to make clear all the inadequacies of her characters and the moral lesson to be learned from them. Repentance in Emma is delayed to the last and therefore most effective moment, and it comes after a train of thought in which we see Emma affected, involved, pressed into realization of her follies. On top of understanding comes marriage, a right resolution to the plot in that it enforces the significance of true understanding. The preparation is over and by extending the novel indefinitely by a closing sentence referring to 'the perfect happiness of the union' Jane Austen assures us that it is an effective understanding that Emma has come to.

These final effects are so precisely controlled and placed that it is evident that we *do* have a plot in which 'composition, distribution and arrangement' are handled with the greatest finesse. It is reached through such indirect methods that one can't but wonder at the vast number of threads that need to be woven into the resolution. The most complex strategy of the novel is the device of filtering it through the eyes of a character of whom Jane Austen doesn't wholly approve, yet with whom she is strongly in sympathy. There is no unsureness about the moments of understanding and improvement that must (despite her position as heroine) come to her. The device is handled particularly by the use of Mr Knightley as a 'corrective'; but that is by no means the whole of the effect, for Mr Knightley is not always right either. Another force exists to handle this; it resides in the values that emerge when we have taken away the irony from the treatment of events seen through Emma's eyes. For we must be careful to see that Emma is right sometimes; we must know, however, precisely when she is wrong. How well this is managed! Emma judges excessively by elegance; but though her criticism of Mrs Elton is that she lacks elegance she perceives most of her faults. Indeed Emma is by no means consistently in error; she is clever enough to be right on nearly all the occasions where she is not giving rein to her snobbery and her prejudice—or pre-judgment. It is Mrs Elton's snobbery that makes Emma's seem mild; and we need the scene where the two talk together to place Emma in that good light. The point then is that if Emma were judged by Jane Austen from 'outside', she would be unlikeable and highly criticized. In fact she is a violator of Jane Austen's moral scale to such a degree that it is hard at first to understand how she could have been made a heroine by her. And the fact that she *is* the heroine is the most remarkable thing about her— *Emma* is Jane Austen's *Tom Jones* in which the most devout expectation roused in the reader is the expectation that she will in some way come to grief; but we demand that her grief, like Tom Jones's, will not be too painful, that repentance will occur, redemption be won and all the blessings of the prodigal son be given to her. This is what happens. The artistic problem of the book is then to make us care for Emma in such a way that we care about her fate, and like her, but that we in no way subdue our moral feelings about her faults.

And here another aspect of the tone is involved. For *Emma* is a comic novel, a novel concerned with comedy of manners in such a way as to make this the comedy of morals. There is comedy in various veins. There is the straightforward humorous treatment of Mr Woodhouse and Miss Bates as 'comic characters'. This, of course, does function in the moral dimension of the book—Mr Woodhouse's affectations are based on an indulgence to himself and it is an indulgence of the same order that has harmed Emma, while Miss

Bates's absurdities make her a kind of test-case for Emma's power of responding to other people. But the significant action of the comedy in the management of the plot is to be found, for example, in the comic flavour of the scenes at the beginning where Emma, Harriet and Mr Elton are playing at picture-making and with riddles. These scenes are treated lightly, and they are designedly about trivial events; but they are organized to show us one thing above all, that Emma is capable of misreading radically the significance of these situations. What makes them most comic to the reader is his sense of a completely different possible explanation for Mr Elton's actions. The operative principle is, in short, an irony that works against the heroine.

This irony dominates the novel. It is contrived through the device of an omniscient narrator who is able to offer an alternative set of values, and it concerns almost always the difference between what the character sees and comes to judgment about, and other potential readings of the incident. It refers then particularly to Emma's habit of prejudging situations. It is offered by a variety of methods, such as the changes in point of view that—for example—let us, at the beginning of Chapter 20, see Jane Fairfax independently of Emma's judging eye. Its effect is not simply to set up another set of *facts* against which Emma's foolish interpretations are judged; we have to wait a while for *those*. What, at the time, we are invited to realize is not that Emma is wrong, but that she might be—that she has prejudged. In short, then, we are drawn away from a determined interpretation or prejudice about people and events, and towards a sense of possible variety. The irony is thus in favour of empiricism; and the pattern of the book is one in which the events presented before us are capable of more complex interpretation. And because we commonly see through Emma's eyes, and because Emma doesn't see this further interpretation, it is dramatically delayed and becomes the centre of our sustained interest. The devices which assure us that it is there are, among other things, the insistent and critical presence of Mr Knightley, the occasional movements to other points of view, and the revelation of the first part that Emma has been wrong about Harriet Smith and so can be wrong again. This tension between events as they seem and events as they might be—between the pleasing Frank Churchill that Emma sees, and the temporizing and cunning Churchill that Mr Knightley sees—is the dynamic of the book. When Churchill comes to Randalls and talks so pleasantly, pleasing everyone, we wonder, we have been prepared to wonder, whether this is because he is deeply amiable or simply cunning. Events will bear at least two interpretations. But it should be said that Emma suspects this, that her views put to Mr Knightley are views she doubts, and that to some extent she has learned from the Harriet incident. As readers, however, skilled in plots, we are put into the position of being encouraged to entertain our suspicions longer; there is a devised relationship between reader and heroine, inherent in the ironic note.

The novel closes on a final irony. One of Emma's faults has been her external view of persons, and her willingness to interfere in the destinies of others without being prepared to involve herself. Marriages are to be made only for others. In being forced into true feelings of love, she is released and opened out; love is the final testimony, in fact, of her redemption. She concludes the book by involving herself in the essential commitment of the Austen universe, which is marriage; so she has opened out into tenderness of heart, a tenderness without weakness or sentimentality. If she has still some faults to recant, these will come in time, for the fundamental liberation has taken place; she is no longer the Sleeping Beauty.

And in this way the shape of the novel is fulfilled. It has begun by delineating a variety of contesting moral viewpoints; it ends by clarification, by offering to the reader his way through the variety. We have learned this particularly through our understanding of Emma's faults, and by learning above all how significant, how *fundamental*, they are. For Emma's aloof relation to others, her willingness to treat them as toys or counters, her over-practical view of the good quality, which she sees simply as ensuring for its possessor a good match—these become significant betrayals of human possibility. 'With insufferable vanity she had believed herself in the secret of everybody's feelings; with unpardonable arrogance proposed to arrange everybody's destiny. She was proved to have been universally mistaken; and she had not quite done nothing—for she had done mischief. She had brought evil on Harriet, on herself, and, she too much feared, on Mr Knightley...' The social and moral universe I described at the beginning of these comments takes on all the weight of its significance here, for it provides a context in which Emma's faults are not peccadilloes to be regarded with indulgence, but total violations of a whole worthwhile universe. Jane Austen's method is to rouse our expectations and draw on our moral stringency to such an extent that this insight becomes absolutely essential, and retribution is demanded. The agents of retribution here are Mr Knightley and Jane Austen herself, and the retribution, once understanding has come, is genial—the lesson learned by Emma is that of how to commit herself fully and properly in the moral and social act of marriage, an act whose validity she has begun by denying and with which she begins her mature life. And what is rendered for us, then, is the moral horror of values we are awfully apt to associate with Jane Austen herself—snobbery, an excessive regard for the elegant and smart, a practical regard for goodness because it is such a *marriageable* trait. These are the values that are purged. We have been turned another way; we have learned of the duty of the individual to immerse himself in the events about him and to accept his obligations to his acquaintance finely and squarely; we have learned of the value of 'the serious spirit', involved and totally responsible. We have been persuaded in fact of the importance of true regard for self and others, persuaded to see the full human being as full, fine, morally serious, totally responsible, entirely involved, and to consider every human action as a crucial, committing act of self-definition.

Critical Quarterly, Vol. 4, 1962, pp. 335–46.

The Difficult Beauty of
Mansfield Park

From the Reverend James Stanier Clarke on, there have been those who see no problem in *Mansfield Park;* it is a pleasing tale of virtue rewarded, and this is enough. But such readers are happily rarer today than a hundred years ago; some of our best critical minds have boggled at accepting Fanny Price and Jane Austen's endorsement of her,[1] and the novel's difficulties have to be faced. Even its admirers have had to season their praise—often for 'technical' successes—with uneasy confessions that its moral frame may be simpler than the fictional life it controls and judges.[2] Only Lionel Trilling observes that such uneasiness marks the prime virtue of the novel, whose greatness is 'commensurate with its power to offend.'[3] One learns more about *Mansfield Park* from Mr Trilling than from anyone else; but while I share his belief in its greatness, I must confess some doubts about his way of reading it. Although Fanny is indeed conceived ironically, I think Jane Austen likes her and wants us to like her too—and despite Mr Trilling's invocation of 'the shade of Pamela', I find it quite

[1] For good statements of the case against the novel, see: D. W. Harding, 'Regulated Hatred,' *Scrutiny*, Vol. VIII, 1940, pp. 346–62; C. S. Lewis, 'A Note on Jane Austen,' *Essays in Criticism*, Vol. IV, 1954, pp. 359–71; and the pertinent chapter in Marvin Mudrick, *Jane Austen: Irony as Defense and Discovery*, Princeton, 1952. Mr Mudrick's is the most uncompromising condemnation, and the most carefully analytical; my reading (and, I suspect, Lionel Trilling's too) was in large part arrived at by trying to answer his objections, and I take this to indicate how vigorous and intelligent his case is, even though I almost entirely disagree with it.

All quotations from *Mansfield Park* are from the edition of R. W. Chapman, 2nd ed., Oxford, 1926; I give page references to this edition, and (in roman numerals) chapter references to the numerous other editions which (unlike Dr Chapman's) number the chapters consecutively, without regard for the original three-volume form.

[2] See, for example, Reginald Farrer, 'Jane Austen,' *Quarterly Review*, Vol. CCXXVIII, 1917, pp. 1–30; Joseph M. Duffy, Jr., 'Moral Integrity and Moral Anarchy in *Mansfield Park*,' *ELH*, Vol. XXIII, 1956, pp. 71–91; Charles Murrah, 'The Background of *Mansfield Park*,' in *From Jane Austen to Joseph Conrad*, ed. R. C. Rathburn and Martin Steinmann, Jr., Minneapolis, 1958, pp. 23–34; and Andrew H. Wright, *Jane Austen's Novels*, rev. ed. London, 1961, pp. 123–34.

[3] Lionel Trilling, '*Mansfield Park*,' in *The Opposing Self*, London and New York, 1955. My dissents from Mr Trilling's views will not, of course, disguise the extent of my indebtedness to his indispensable essay.

possible to do so. Nor can I accept his view of Henry and Mary Crawford; surely they are presented consistently, and with entire persuasiveness, as being more gravely flawed and less charming than he finds them, even at first reading; and in Mary, especially, Jane Austen diagnoses a moral disorder that, because less under conscious control, is both more alarming and more pitiful than the *deliberate* insincerities and impersonations with which he charges them. In short, Mr Trilling concedes too much to the opposition, even to the extent of accepting the idea that the novel's praise 'is not for social freedom but for social stasis', that it rejects 'spiritedness, vivacity, celerity, and lightness . . . as having nothing to do with virtue and happiness'. Fanny and Edmund do reject freedom and vivacity, to be sure, and they are right to do so, considering who they are, but Jane Austen's view of the rejection is considerably more complicated and troubled than theirs. *Mansfield Park* does speak, as Mr Trilling says, 'to our secret inexpressible hopes' of escaping the 'demands of personality' and secular complexity, but it warns as well that such an escape would cost us dearly.

It is first of all a singularly 'beautiful' novel, one in which Jane Austen draws more than usual upon 'scenic' resources.[4] We attend more to where people are and what they are doing, and, more important, scenery makes fuller contact with moral meaning. The excursion to Sotherton reveals this mingling of scene and meaning at its fullest. In contravention of Mrs Norris' plans for organized sightseeing,

> the young people, meeting with an outward door, temptingly open on a flight of steps which led immediately to turf and shrubs, and all the sweets of pleasure-grounds, as by one impulse, one wish for air and liberty, all walked out (p. 90, ix).

The tangled syntax reflects another entanglement, of motive and evaluation, which the setting expresses too: it is good to thwart Mrs Norris and all *calculations* about pleasure, yet the 'impulse' seems too easily satisfied, the 'sweets' too 'immediate'. (Are not gardens 'tempting' places?) Guests should wait for invitations, but more than good manners seems at issue. There follows a dance-like movement through the landscape of lawn, Wilderness, and park, in which personal groupings, and the romantic possibilities they imply, dissolve and reform; Henry and Maria slip into the locked park, jealously followed by Julia and Rushworth; Mary and Edmund rejoin a lonely Fanny and are welcomed back by Authority in an amusingly theatrical tableau: 'on [their] reaching the bottom of the steps to the terrace, Mrs Rushworth and Mrs Norris presented themselves at the top' (p. 103, x).

---

[4] This is the point of Mr Murrah's essay; both he and Mr Duffy say that the Sotherton episode is important.

Happily, it is not the novelist but the characters who seek to exploit the scene's obvious symbolic possibilities. Mary, for one, has a lively sense of what might be done with the landscape:

'We have taken such a very serpentine course; and the wood itself must be half a mile long in a straight line, for we have never seen the end of it yet, since we left the first great path.'

'But if you remember, before we left that first great path, we saw directly to the end of it. We looked down the whole vista, and saw it closed by iron gates, and it could not have been more than a furlong in length.'

'Oh! I know nothing of your furlongs, but I am sure it is a very long wood; and that we have been winding in and out ever since we came. . . .'

'We have been exactly a quarter of an hour here,' said Edmund, taking out his watch. 'Do you think we are walking four miles an hour?'

'Oh! do not attack me with your watch. A watch is always too fast or too slow. I cannot be dictated to by a watch' (pp. 94–5, ix).

Mary wants the Wilderness to be a Forest of Love (or at least Dalliance); her terms—serpentine course, first great path, not seeing to the end of it—playfully hint at an allegory of possible emotional involvement. She aims at a charming 'femininity', but her projection of the scene as a Spenserian forest where time and space are suspended seems strained and coy. If Edmund (as so often) misses the point with his blundering addition of the iron gates and his inept insistence on furlongs and watches, we must still agree that time and space do exist, both as they affect people (Fanny is tired) and in their resonances as moral metaphors—to romanticize like this is to risk losing your bearings.

The danger becomes clear when Henry and Maria stand foiled by the gate:

'Your prospects, however, are too fair to justify want of spirits. You have a very smiling scene before you.'

'Do you mean literally or figuratively? Literally, I conclude. Yes, certainly, the sun shines and the park looks very cheerful. But unluckily that iron gate, that ha-ha, gives me a feeling of restraint and hardship. I cannot get out, as the starling said.' As she spoke, and it was with expression, she walked to the gate; he followed her. 'Mr Rushworth is so long fetching this key!'

'And for the world you would not get out without the key and without Mr Rushworth's authority and protection, or I think you might with little difficulty pass round the edge of the gate, here, with my assistance; I think it might be done, if you really wished to be more at large, and could allow yourself to think it not prohibited.'

'Prohibited! nonsense! I certainly can get out that way, and I will' (p. 99, x).

This innuendo-ridden talk is what Edmund's stolid belief in time and space unwittingly saved him from. Jane Austen predicts the final disaster of Maria and Henry, but the moment evokes views of obligation and licence that are more than aspects of 'plot' or 'character' Freedom is tempting *because* it may be wicked. Each—Henry slyly, Maria impetuously—uses the setting to mirror improper interest in the other; since neither admits that the conversation is 'figurative', they can dally with perfect efficiency (for both, getting into the park easily becomes 'getting *out*') without taking any responsibility for their insinuations. People who imply that they mean more than they say, yet refuse to say what they mean, are both irritating and dishonest, and Fanny, though as usual she can't quite say it, senses thoroughly what is at stake: 'you will certainly hurt yourself against those spokes—you will tear your gown—you will be in danger of slipping into the ha-ha. You had better not go.' Setting becomes the image of moral violence.

The whole episode is beautifully drawn, but like other great moments in *Mansfield Park* it represents more than a local triumph of 'technique', to be weighed against a pervasive failure of discrimination and understanding by the author. The beauty of the novel, its brilliant combining of Jane Austen's usual mastery of speech and incident with a new sense of what setting can express, serves the end of a subtler statement and development of the novelist's grasp of the fictional 'life' she deals with. Though it would be hard to prove, I think we are *told* less in this novel than in her others; evaluations are less clear-cut, judgments less reliant on any moral schematism, significance more dependent on our 'reading' of scenes. If we look in Fanny for the signs that so firmly place Jane Austen's other heroines we will not find them, nor are Edmund, Mary, and Henry so distinctly given moral location. But this blurring of the outlines of comedy of manners (or fairytale)⁵ creates not confusion but a new generosity and seriousness in the presentation of 'theme'.

The theme presented has to do with meddling, seeking to impose one's will on creatures entitled to wills of their own, treating other lives as though one's designs for them were their chief reason for being. Stated so broadly, this is the theme of *Emma* and, if less prominently, of the other novels too; at this level of generality, indeed, it is the theme of most classic fiction and many of our difficulties

⁵ Both Mr Harding and Mr Lewis suggest Cinderella as a pattern for Fanny Price. But Edmund, her reward for suffering, is hardly a Prince Charming; it is the Crawfords, not Jane Austen, who impose fantasy upon truth.

with life. But in *Mansfield Park* it gets a fullness of treatment not to be equalled until the triumphs of George Eliot and James.[6]

There is first Mrs Norris, whose selfish meddling is the novelist's hint of deeper significance elsewhere. Miss Lascelles remarks that her favourite phrase is 'between ourselves', 'with its suggestions of conspiracy and wire-pulling';[7] to this might be added the set of variations—'I perfectly comprehend you,' 'I entirely agree with you,' 'that is exactly what I think,' etc.—that at least once reveals its theme: 'If I were you' (p. 55, vi). Mrs Norris, in other ways demonstrably Jane Austen's most nearly psychotic creation, yearns to merge with other existences, and she deeply resents resistance:

> [Fanny] likes to go her own way to work; she does not like to be dictated to; she takes her own independent walk whenever she can; she certainly has a little spirit of secrecy and independence, and nonsense, about her, which I would advise her to get the better of (p. 323, xxxii).

Although Sir Thomas, recently guilty of the same view, thinks this unjust, Mrs Norris has put her finger on something. Behind her softness of manner, Fanny does indeed resist, and her aunt's sense of this impels her astounding attempt virtually to *become* Fanny:

> Depend upon it, it is not you that are wanted; depend upon it it is me (looking at the butler) but you are so very eager to put yourself forward. What should Sir Thomas want you for? It is me, Baddeley, you mean; I am coming this moment. You mean me, Baddeley, I am sure; Sir Thomas wants me, not Miss Price (p. 325, xxxii).

For an appalling moment, her madness reveals itself not simply as a yearning for intimacy with Sir Thomas's power but as a desperate hunger for the identities of other people, even the most insignificant.

But the contagion is wider spread. Tom Bertram's peevish complaint about Mrs Norris—'it raises my spleen more than any thing, to have the pretence of being asked, of being given a choice, and at the same time addressed in such a way as to oblige one to do the very thing' (p. 120, xii)—reveals, as Fanny sees, *his* will to have his own way, as when by extravagance he cheerfully deprived Edmund of half his income or tried to bully Fanny into joining the company of *Lovers' Vows* ('Let her choose for herself as well as the rest of us,' Edmund had then to urge him). Lady Bertram is in her own vegetable way quite as selfish as her sister and daughters; Sir Thomas sadly comes

---

[6] Barbara B. Collins, 'Jane Austen's Victorian Novel,' *Nineteenth-Century Fiction*, Vol. IV, 1949, pp. 175–85, recognizes that *Mansfield Park* anticipates some of the methods of Victorian fiction, but in her view it is 'a forerunner of the dowdy propriety and piety which blossomed in the 'fifties'.

[7] Mary Lascelles, *Jane Austen and Her Art*, Oxford, 1939, p. 164.

to see that he has spoiled his family not only by indulgence but by repressing their moral freedom; even Edmund attempts to urge Fanny into Henry's arms. Robbing people of their choice lies at the heart of virtually every significant incident in the novel.

Something disturbingly more than a lack of sincerity vitiates the charm of the Crawfords. We notice that Henry is attracted to Fanny as to a puzzle:

> I do not quite know what to make of Miss Fanny. I do not understand her. I could not tell what she would be at yesterday.... I must try to get the better of this. Her looks say, 'I will not like you, I am determined not to like you,' and I say, she shall (p. 230, xxiv).

Lawrence would know what to make of this hunger for 'knowing', this will to destroy another's separateness. Henry is of course more than a Lovelace, and his 'moral taste' is sufficient to appreciate Fanny's capacity for feeling, but the growth of his love gets consistent qualification:

> It would be something to be loved by such a girl, to excite the first ardours of her young, unsophisticated mind! (p. 235, xxiv).

> [His vanity] convinced him that he should be able in time to make [her] feelings what he wished.... [His love] made her affection appear of greater consequence, because it was withheld, and determined him to have the glory, as well as the felicity, of forcing her to love him (p. 326, xxxiii).

His will to dominate, to recreate the world as an image of his wishes, keeps him from ever quite recognizing her reality as 'another'. Nor is this a matter of the narrator imposing a commentary on Henry that his speech and behaviour won't support; when, for example, Mary doubts that Fanny would much appreciate their dissolute uncle, Henry can airily reply that 'he is a very good man, and has been more than a father to me. Few fathers would have let me have my own way half so much. You must not prejudice Fanny against him. I must have them love one another' (p. 296, xxx). It is not moral imperception—his tone suggests some amusement about both his uncle and himself—but his determination that both Fanny and the Admiral shall be objects to manipulate that defines the irony.

Mary is a richer figure, subject to more complex attention and concern, but she too shows a corruption by will. As in her dismissal of time and space at Sotherton, she likes to imagine worlds more congenial than the real one. Edmund's simple determination to be ordained seems to her (pp. 227–8, xxiii) a deliberate insult, shattering her trust in a different, imaginary future: 'It was plain now that he could have no serious views, no true attachment, by fixing himself in a situation which he must know she would never stoop to.' She suffers from not being able to strike back at Sir Thomas, the presumed 'destroyer' of her 'agreeable fancies'—'not daring to relieve herself by a single attempt at throwing ridicule on his cause' (p. 248, xxv). As for any child, what others do has always direct reference to herself, as when she equates Edmund's 'adhering to his own notions' with 'acting on them in defiance of her' (p. 286, xxix). This wilfulness must, to be sure, be weighed against her appreciation of Edmund himself (as well as her dream of him as a 'man of independent fortune') and against her ability to rebuke herself: 'She was afraid she had used some strong—some contemptuous expressions in speaking of the clergy, and *that* should not have been. It was ill-bred—it was wrong. She wished such words unsaid with all her heart' (p. 286, xxix). The dashes indicate the difficult achievement of honesty, as she resists the tempting understatements of her fault. She engages more of our sympathetic interest than her brother, but Mary, rather more gravely than Emma Woodhouse, is prey to what Jane Austen's revered Dr Johnson called 'the dangerous prevalence of imagination'.

Only Fanny recognizes the perils of will, in resisting Edmund's advancement of Henry as a fit object for her reforming powers:

'I would not engage in such a charge,' cried Fanny in a shrinking accent—'in such an office of high responsibility!'

'As usual, believing yourself unequal to anything!—fancying everything too much for you!' (p. 351, xxxv).

Edmund seldom appreciates subtlety; far from 'fancying', Fanny here recognizes both the difficulty and the impropriety of disturbing the existences of other people, however bad. She comes as close as she can to explaining this when Henry seeks to draw her into intimacy by soliciting her advice:

'When you give me your opinion, I always know what is right. Your judgment is my rule of right.'

'Oh, no!—do not say so. We have all a better guide in ourselves, if we would attend to it, than any other person can be' (p. 412, xlii).

The reader who thinks Conscience a quaint concept is (as he deserves to be) in trouble here. Fanny's inner guide is her only defence against will, her own or someone else's. *Mansfield Park,* a novel without miracles, has no instance of one character converting another by sitting down for a good, serious talk. Rather, those who have a conscience, like Edmund and Sir Thomas, work out their salvations in the quiet privacy of their own thoughts, while those who have none, like Henry and Mrs Norris, or who cannot find the privacy to listen to theirs, like Mary and Maria, find no refuge from the desolations that the will insists on. . . .

Sense and Sensibility:
A Mixed-Up Book

...*Mansfield Park* is a book divided against itself. So is *Sense and Sensibility*: and it is worth mentioning that (after *Emma*, the undoubted masterpiece) these are the two most powerful and disturbing of the novels. *Pride and Prejudice* may be a more perfect work of art, but it does not touch us to the quick as can these two mixed-up books. *Sense and Sensibility* is mixed-up in the most radical way imaginable. It is meant to be a comedy in which we come to realize the superiority of Sense: we are to be fond of Marianne, but we are to smile at her, and we are to see that Elinor's restraint and wisdom are more valuable than her emotionalism. And so Marianne makes her appearance as someone we are not to take wholly seriously: we are told that Colonel Brandon appears to her 'an absolute old bachelor, for he was on the wrong side of five and thirty' and if we know that she is eventually to marry him we smile. When she sings at the Middletons, he is the only one who listens to her:

> His pleasure in music, though it amounted not to that ecstatic delight which alone could sympathize with her own, was estimable when contrasted against the horrible insensibility of the others; and she was reasonable enough to allow that a man of five and thirty might well have outlived all acuteness of feeling and every exquisite power of enjoyment. She was perfectly disposed to make every allowance for the colonel's advanced state of life which humanity required (Chap. VII).

This is how Marianne is treated before the appearance of Willoughby and right at the end of the book she is married off in the same tone:

> Marianne Dashwood was born to an extraordinary fate. She was born to discover the falsehood of her own opinions, and to counteract, by her conduct, her most favourite maxims. She was born to overcome an affection formed so late in life as at seventeen, and with no sentiment superior to strong esteem and lively friendship, voluntarily to give her hand to another!—and *that* other, a man who had suffered no less than herself under the event of a former attachment, whom two years before, she had considered too old to be

married,—and who still sought the constitutional safeguard of a flannel waistcoat (Chap. i).

The tone of this, surely, is not quite right: the tone, or its content. 'No sentiment superior to strong esteem and lively friendship': does Jane Austen then not believe in love? Does the love which is based on gratitude and esteem turn out simply to *be* gratitude and esteem? And that last old-maidish joke about the flannel waistcoat: can we not hear too audibly the relief that marriage is not going to contain anything excessive, anything violent, anything common?

Yet on its own the paragraph is not likely to jar; and it would not jar if we turned straight to it after reading the first eight chapters. For *Sense and Sensibility* begins as pure comedy, and continues so for eight chapters, chapters of unmixed delight. If we are disturbed at finding this note at the end, it is because we have in the meantime read the tragedy of Marianne.

> 'Oh! Elinor,' she cried, 'you have made me hate myself for ever. How barbarous have I been to you!—you, who have been my only comfort, who have borne with me in all my misery, who have seemed to be only suffering for me!—is this my gratitude? Is this the only return I can make you? Because your merit cries out upon myself, I have been trying to do it away.' (Chap. xxxvi).

Such an outburst shatters the shell of comedy, and puts Marianne in front of us as a suffering woman, not affecting sensibility, but feeling passion; and it is not an isolated moment, but a carefully prepared climax. For the thirty-nine central chapters of the book she has been learning her lessons too painfully for banter.

And by not remaining a comedy *Sense and Sensibility* fails in its professed aim: it does not succeed in winning us to the side of Sense. The two faults are one. Jane Austen set herself the task of making fun of Marianne, and engaging sympathy for Elinor: if sympathy for Marianne becomes too violent, if Marianne more than Elinor seems to embody the book's positives, then we shall not be led to the intended conclusion. And this is what happens: Marianne, in the intense seriousness with which she is presented, engages our sympathy at a level that makes us want to locate the positives in *her*:

> This was the season of happiness to Marianne. Her heart was devoted to Willoughby, and the fond attachment to Norland which she brought with her from Sussex, was more likely to be softened than she had thought it possible before, by the charms which his society bestowed on her present home (Chap. xi).

The gentle, leisurely second sentence could have been written of Elinor: but not the blunt brief opening sentence. Its immediacy, its impulsive directness—this is the way Marianne is spoken of, and Marianne only.

To illustrate what I mean by saying that Marianne embodies the strongest positives in the book, I must quote at length. The Dashwood sisters—like all Jane Austen heroines—have to spend a good deal of their time in the company of malicious and importunate women. Elinor finds it hard to put up with the Misses Steele: for Lucy Steele confides in her in order to gratify her envy, and Ann is a nuisance through sheer stupidity. The Misses Steele call in the middle of Marianne's grief and the elder says 'I am sorry we cannot see your sister, Miss Dashwood. I am sorry she is not well.' Elinor does her best to put her off, but the silly woman insists that Marianne will see 'such old friends as Lucy and me'.

> Elinor, with great civility, declined the proposal. 'Her sister was perhaps laid down upon the bed, or in her dressing-gown, and therefore not able to come to them.'
> 'Oh, if that's all,' cried Miss Steele, 'we can just as well go and see *her.*'
> Elinor began to find this impertinence too much for her temper; but she was saved the trouble of checking it, by Lucy's sharp reprimand (Chap. xxxii).

The effect of such episodes is to feed our irritation. We too find the impertinence (of the Steele sisters, of Mrs Ferrars, of Fanny Dashwood) too much for our tempers, and as we move through the book our impatience mounts, our need to put a check to this constant and insensitive insolence. And then comes an episode in which the irritation is released. At the dinner party which the Dashwoods give in Chapter xxxiv, almost all the ill-will and cattiness in the book is gathered together. As the gentlemen enter the drawing-room, they notice, and admire, a pair of screens that Elinor has painted for her sister-in-law; the screens are passed round, and justify their presence in the novel by the rich variety of comments they excite. [Chap. xxxiv, 'Mrs Ferrars, not aware of their being Elinor's work . . . a sister slighted in the smallest point.' Please read through the passage.]
. . . No quotation could be long enough to convey the effect of this moment when we come upon it: for the tension that Marianne releases has been building up not only all through dinner, but all through the visit to London—indeed, all through the book. When Elinor feels such an impulse, she bottles it up, or is saved by circumstances from uttering it; but now at last Marianne has spoken to one of these vicious old women as they deserve. No one else would have done it, for those two patterns of masculine behaviour, Edward Ferrars and Colonel Brandon, are impeccable in observing propriety; and where propriety demands restraint (as it usually does), restraint there will be. Colonel Brandon may be endangering Marianne's happiness if he doesn't reveal the horrid truth about Willoughby, but he has no right to speak, so he resists the improper impulse. The tension in this scene has built

up so strongly because of Jane Austen's unique combination of truth-telling and acceptance. Jane Austen is a conservative in manners, and doesn't want impropriety from her sympathetic characters; but such propriety assumes a certain evasiveness (Elinor is the one on whom 'the whole task of telling lies when politeness required it always fell'), and is undermined by the ruthless analysis that the novels offer. So when at last Marianne allows her impulses to follow where the satiric analysis has pointed—when she yields to rudeness and snaps at Mrs Ferrars—the whole novel has been straining towards the assent we give her.

But if *Sense and Sensibility* is inviting us to feel as Marianne does about Mrs Ferrars, it is also urging us to condemn the expression of such feeling. Convention and truthtelling—the conservatism of propriety and the radicalism of satire—jostle unreconciled in the last paragraph of this quotation. Jane Austen's own comment is probably Elinor's, who 'was much more hurt by Marianne's warmth, than she had been by what produced it'; but if we want to cry shame on Elinor, we can do so with Colonel Brandon, blinded by love into transcending his author's preferences.

Marianne, says Marvin Mudrick, is 'the life and centre of the book'; and the most brilliant chapter of his book on Jane Austen defends her against her creator. I will not repeat his arguments, but I will consider the reply we might have expected Jane Austen to make. This is that we are wrong to contrast a passionate Marianne with a prudent Elinor, for Elinor too has her passions: only she has the wisdom to control them. 'She had an excellent heart; her disposition was affectionate, and her feelings were strong: but she knew how to govern them.' That at the beginning of the book; and at the end the mother comes to acknowledge 'that in Elinor she might have a daughter suffering almost as much, certainly with less self-provocation, and greater fortitude'. So when Marianne, having discovered that Elinor's love affair has been going as badly as hers, suggests that her self-command has been made easier because she does not feel much, she is corrected in a long eloquent speech ('the composure of mind with which I have brought myself at present to consider the matter, the consolation that I have been willing to admit, have been the effect of constant and painful exertion') that wrings from Marianne the self-reproach quoted above. Nothing could make the book's intention plainer than that: and perhaps nothing could at the same time defeat the intention so clearly. Elinor is eloquent, but Marianne is moved; and in the very moment of admitting that she has wronged her sister by under-estimating her suffering, she speaks with the accent of suffering herself; an accent we never hear from Elinor.

For it is not enough that Jane Austen should tell us that Elinor feels deeply: she must convince us as an artist, not merely announce an intention. Her failure seems due to one cause above all others:

that when Elinor's strong feelings are mentioned, this is almost invariably accompanied by an assurance that she was able to govern them:

> 'I did,' said Elinor, with a composure of voice under which was concealed an emotion and distress beyond anything she had ever felt before. She was mortified, shocked, confounded (Chap. xxii).

The composure of voice is almost always there. This is unwise rhetoric on Jane Austen's part; and the result is that it is hard for us to believe in these strong feelings: as we hear them so continually linked to the successful effort to control them, to smile, to conceal what it would be improper to betray, we can hardly credit them with a separate existence.

I know of only one moment when Elinor's emotion rings as true as Marianne's, and it occurs in Marianne's great tragic scene, of the reception of Willoughby's letter.

> Again they were both silent. Elinor was employed in walking thoughtfully from the fire to the window, from the window to the fire, without knowing that she received warmth from one, or discerning objects through the other; and Marianne, seated at the foot of the bed, with her head leaning against one of its posts, again took up Willoughby's letter, and after shuddering over every sentence, exclaimed—(Chap. xxix).

Here for once Elinor's grief seems the more genuine of the two: it is Marianne who uses rhetoric, Elinor who is presented in the physical immediacy of her sorrow. And even this paragraph probably does her less good than it should in our eyes: for it is not her own grief that is in question, but her sharing of Marianne's, and coming in the midst of Marianne's tragedy, it probably rests in the mind as a reflex from that, rather than as Elinor's very own emotion.

The true heroine of *Sense and Sensibility* is Marianne; and her true conquest is not over Colonel Brandon but over the propriety in whose name the author puts her down. The result is that a perfect comedy of manners was spoilt, and a great flawed novel written. . . .

The Truthtellers: Jane Austen, George Eliot, D. H. Lawrence, London, 1967, pp. 160–6.

Select Bibliography

STANDARD EDITION OF JANE AUSTEN'S WORKS:

The Novels, ed. R. W. Chapman, 5 vols, Oxford, 1923, 2nd ed. 1926.
Minor Works, ed. R. W. Chapman, London, 1954.
Two Chapters of 'Persuasion', ed. R. W. Chapman, Oxford, 1926.

BIBLIOGRAPHY:

G. L. Keynes, *Jane Austen: A Bibliography*, London, 1929.
R. W. Chapman, *Jane Austen: A Critical Bibliography*, Oxford, 1953, 2nd ed. 1955.

LETTERS AND BIOGRAPHY:

Jane Austen: Letters to her Sister Cassandra and Others, ed. R. W. Chapman, 2 vols, Oxford, 1932, 2nd ed. 1952.
James Edward Austen-Leigh, *A Memoir of Jane Austen*, London, 1870; ed. R. W. Chapman, Oxford, 1926.
Constance Hill, *Jane Austen: Her Homes and Her Friends*, London, 1902; 3rd ed. 1923.
W. and R. A. Austen-Leigh, *Jane Austen, Her Life and Letters, A Family Record*, London, 1913.
Elizabeth Jenkins, *Jane Austen: A Biography*, London, 1938, repr. 1948.

CRITICAL WORKS: (*In addition* to those books and articles from which extracts have been given in this anthology.)

(a) *BOOKS:*

Howard S. Babb, *Jane Austen's Novels: The Fabric of Dialogue*, Ohio, 1962.
Frank W. Bradbrook, *Jane Austen: Emma*, (Studies in English Literature 3), London, 1961.
Jane Austen and Her Predecessors, Cambridge, 1966.
R. W. Chapman, *Jane Austen: Facts and Problems*, Oxford, 1948.
W. A. Craik, *Jane Austen: The Six Novels*, London, 1965.
Avrom Fleishman, *A Reading of 'Mansfield Park': An Essay in Critical Synthesis*, Minneapolis, 1967.
Robert Liddell, *The Novels of Jane Austen*, London, 1963.
A. W. Litz, *Jane Austen: A Study of Her Artistic Development*, London, 1965.
Norman Sherry, *Jane Austen*, (Literature in Perspective), London, 1966.
B. C. Southam, *Jane Austen's Literary Manuscripts: A Study of the Novelist's Development through the Surviving Papers*, Oxford, 1964.
(ed.) *Jane Austen: The Critical Heritage*, London, 1968. [All significant criticism up to 1870.]
(ed.) *Critical Essays on Jane Austen*, London, 1968.

Andrew Wright, *Jane Austen's Novels: A Study in Structure*, London, 1953; 2nd ed. 1961.

(b) *ESSAYS AND ARTICLES:*

Kingsley Amis, 'What Became of Jane Austen? *Mansfield Park*', *Spectator*, Vol. CIC, 1957, pp. 339–40.

Wayne Booth, 'Control of Distance in Jane Austen's *Emma*', in *The Rhetoric of Fiction*, Chicago, 1961.

Frank W. Bradbrook, 'Style and Judgment in Jane Austen's Novels', *Cambridge Journal*, Vol. IV, 1951, pp. 515–37.

'The Letters of Jane Austen', *Cambridge Journal*, Vol. VII, 1954, pp. 259–76.

Janet Burroway, 'The Irony of the Insufferable Prig: *Mansfield Park*,' in *Critical Quarterly*, Vol. 9, no. 2, 1967, pp. 127–38.

Joseph Cady and Ian Watt, 'Jane Austen's Critics', *Critical Quarterly*, Vol. 5, 1963, pp. 49–63.

Barbara B. Collins, 'Jane Austen's Victorian Novel', *Nineteenth-Century Fiction*, Vol. IV, 1949, pp. 175–85.

Joseph M. Duffy, Jr, '*Emma:* The Awakening From Innocence', *English Literary History*, Vol. XXI, 1954, pp. 39–53.

'Moral Integrity and Moral Anarchy in *Mansfield Park*', *English Literary History*, Vol. XXIII, 1956, pp. 71–91.

Christopher Gillie, '*Sense and Sensibility*', *Essays in Criticism*, Vol. IX, 1959, pp. 1–9.

Andor Gomme, 'On not being Persuaded', *Essays in Criticism*, Vol. XVI, 1966, pp. 170–84.

D. W. Harding, 'Jane Austen and Moral Judgment', *Pelican Guide to English Literature*, London, 1957, Vol. V, pp. 51–9.

W. J. Harvey, 'The Plot of *Emma*', in *Essays in Criticism*, Vol. 17, 1967, pp. 48–63.

Charles Beecher Hogan, 'Jane Austen and Her Early Public', *Review of English Studies*, n.s. Vol. I, 1950, pp. 39–54.

Ian Jack, 'The Epistolary Element in Jane Austen', *English Studies Today*, 2nd series, 1961, pp. 173–86.

Arnold Kettle, '*Emma*' in *An Introduction to the English Novel*, London, 1951, Vol. I, pp. 90–104.

J. E. M. Latham, 'Head versus Heart: The Role of Miss Bates in *Emma*', in *English*, Vol. XV, no. 88, 1965, pp. 140–3.

F. R. Leavis, *The Great Tradition*, London, 1948, pp. 1–27.

Q. D. Leavis, 'A Critical Theory of Jane Austen's Writings', *Scrutiny*, Vol. X, 1941–2, pp. 61–87; 114–42; 272–94; Vol. XII, 1944, pp. 104–19.

David Lodge, Chapter on the language in *Emma* in *Language of Fiction*, London, 1966.

Alan D. McKillop, 'Critical Realism in *Northanger Abbey*', *From Jane Austen to Joseph Conrad*, ed. R. C. Rathburn and M. Steinmann, Jr, Minneapolis, 1958, pp. 35–45.

Charles Murrah, 'The Background of *Mansfield Park*', ibid., pp. 23–34.

Mark Schorer, 'Fiction and the Matrix of Analogy', *The Kenyon Review*, Vol. XI, 1949, pp. 539–60.

Edgar F. Shannon, Jr, '*Emma:* Character and Construction', *P.M.L.A.*, Vol. LXXI, pp. 637–50.

B. C. Southam, 'Mrs Leavis and Miss Austen: The "Critical Theory" Reconsidered', *Nineteenth-Century Fiction*, Vol. XVII, 1962, pp. 21–32.

Tony Tanner, Introduction to the Penguin edition of *Mansfield Park*, London, 1966.

Stuart M. Tave, 'Review of Marvin Mudrick's *Jane Austen: Irony as Defense and Discovery*', *Philological Quarterly*, Vol. XXXII, July 1953, pp. 256–7.

Lionel Trilling, '*Mansfield Park*', *Partisan Review*, Vol. XXI, 1954, pp. 492–511; reprinted in *The Opposing Self*, London, 1955, pp. 206–30; also in *Pelican Guide to English Literature*, London, 1957, Vol. V, pp. 112–29.

'*Emma*', *Encounter*, Vol. VIII, 1957, pp. 49–59.

Dorothy Van Ghent, '*Pride and Prejudice*' in *The English Novel: Form and Function*, New York, 1953, pp. 99–111.

Ian Watt, Chapter on Jane Austen in *The Rise of the Novel*, Berkeley, California, 1957.

Edmund Wilson, 'A Long Talk on Jane Austen', in *Classics and Commercials*, London, 1951.